IMANI MEANS FAITH

IMANI MEANS FAITH

Surviving life's harsh realities

IMANI M. WATSON

First Printing, 2020

Dedication

To my mother,
Thank you. Thank you for all of the hidden lessons, even the
ones that didn't feel like lessons, turned out to be essential to my
being. I learned exactly what I needed to, when I needed to.
You've contributed more to who I am than I have been able to
recognize in the past. Through your struggles, I was able to learn
things I wouldn't have gotten from anywhere else. It's easy to be
blinded by pain, but it takes a different kind of fight to push be-
yond that pain. A kind of fight that I learned directly from you
as a mother. You taught me how to fight through any and every-
thing that may land on my plate. You showed me that fear ac-
complishes nothing, but static. You showed me what it means to
be fearless, in a world that creates a suffocating space for Black
women. Now, where would I be without that? In addition to
your strength, you taught me how to pick myself up from the
darkest spaces. You taught me how to stay true to myself. Because
of you, I know how to remain Imani in the face of struggle and
adversity. You created my desire for authenticity. You pushed
me to be a protector and nailed it to my understanding that no
matter what I do, to never stop pushing. Everything I love about
my growth has stemmed directly from your life and lessons.
Neither one of us were afforded gentle upbringings, but our sto-
ries will aid others facing similar struggles. I dedicate this book
to you, not only to highlight growth and possibility, but most im-

portantly, to highlight my deep gratitude and love for you and our journey. I love you, mom (Fredricka).

Imani (Faith): *"To believe with all our heart in the victory of our struggle"*

Prelude: A Hurt Soul

2013: I was raised by experience. This heart of mine has been beaten, worn, raped, & stabbed. These eyes of mine have seen kidnapping, death, & drugs being used by women that were supposed to be paving the way for me. I have had friends f*ck me over & then question my loyalty. Dudes who've took advantage of my heart, mind, & soul without a thought about it. & people ask why I'm so angry or "grown," b*tch the same reason you are blind & too dumb to see that I am emotionally struggling! Everything I am is because of what has happened to me! Nobody taught me that I was special or smart! Nobody taught me how to be loyal or to have my priories in order! Nobody taught me how to love myself & to stay in school! Nobody taught me that niggas will f*ck you in, out, & around & won't be s*it the next day! F*ck a text that says "I'm always here." I've never had a shoulder to drown with these tears, I've never been able to flat-out experience somebody "always" being there, but don't nobody hear me tho. These little ass problems people always stressing over, don't nobody know what it's like to be alive feeling dead as f*ck! Don't nobody know how it feel attempting to take your own life. Then people wanna take me for granted. Do you know what it *takes for me to give somebody REAL love? I give that sh*t to people who has the heart to say f*ck me! Don't nobody ever take into consideration how f*cked up my 18 years of living has went. F*ck the hype of my life & what it looks like, I'm wounded that I had to be grown at 15. This wasn't no fun a** journey. Yeah I got my head on right & I'm headed in the right direction but that sh*t don't delete memories. I still remember every night my mom left for the streets, I still remember every friend that did me in the dirt, I still remember every lie my daddy told me, I still remember EVERY f*cking time I saw my grandma do crack, I still remember every dude that has dogged me, & I still remember every night I couldn't breathe from crying my guts out. So the next time you wanna think I'm always mad or say some shit about how I act? Don't feel bad or like you owe me. Know that I'm thinking F*CK YOU, cause ain't NOBODY help me get to where I am, I could've did it better w/o the fake a** love.*

Chapter 1: Is This Normal?

2/27/2019: You don't recall much of what happened up to the first five to six years of your life. From the bits and pieces you try to put together, from what little you try to remember, from the stories that pictures tell, things were pretty normal. Life did not go on full speed mode until about 15, or maybe it was 13, or that time you were six. Who knows, all that is known is that at some point throughout this thing called life, yours took off at a pace that you lost control of. None of it makes sense to you right now. You question everything life has to offer and sometimes even life itself. You cannot understand for the life of you why you were chosen to live this life. You feel sorry for yourself, something you will eventually learn to let go of. But, not right now. You have not let it go at this moment, and really, you do not have to let it go as you are still a child.

Although sometimes it does not appear this way, you are still a child who needs guidance, who lacks proper decision making skills, and who was forced into believing that you are anything other than a child. Right now you're six. You're six years old and for some reason it feels like life began at this moment. You are left at home with someone you consider a "cousin." You know, one of those cousins who does not share any biological characteristics, but they are present in your life and your moms hang so often that you do not know how else to label each other. You are not friends, you do not have much in common, and had it not been for your parents, you would have probably never crossed paths. But, you did, you crossed paths very early in life and you just called each other, "cousins." You are six years old and this "cousin" is 14 or so. You never knew how much older he was, but you knew that he was in charge of watching you and any other kids in the home at the time. At some point throughout this night you are awakened from your sleep. You are then asked by this cousin to change from the pajamas you put on, to a large white T-shirt. You will not ever forget this white T-shirt. In a way, this T-shirt symbolized the beginning of life for you. Throughout life, as you get older, you will learn to detach from the white T-shirt and place your blame in all the appropriate places. But for now, mourn the T-shirt. Hate it, despise it, and stand up to it. As you feel that is the only way to defend your innocence being taken away. Back to this cousin. You do what he says. You change from Barbie pajamas and into this white T-shirt. Your cousin asks you to leave the room where everyone else had fallen asleep. He takes you to your brother's room where there is no one else and he begins transferring his devilish energy onto you. You lie there and accept what is happening. You do not quite understand why he would want to do this to you, but you do not utter a word. And you won't utter one about this encounter for at least four to five years. You allow this to shape who you are. You allow this to create anger in your heart. You allow this to strip you of the girl you could have been. You even spend years trying to convince yourself that this did not happen. But no time for that, life has started and it will not let up any time soon.

About three years later, you are left home alone with another child of your mom's friend. A different one this time. This one is a girl, so you do not fear at all that anything will happen to you. It is not until maybe 20 years old you will uncover and face the damage done to you on this night. At 20, the image of her, the feeling of her, and the feeling of you urinating on yourself as she is stripping away more of your childhood. It will all come rushing and it will cause you anger and frustration beyond what you would like. You will mourn the true pain of this later in life. You will find the answer to why you always wanted to fight. You will find the answer to why you wet the bed until you were 12. You will find the answer to why you enjoyed "playing house." You will find the answer to why you become intensely focused on school to the exclusion of other activities, or on the other end why it becomes so easy for you to disengage in everything, including school. The sooner you address what happened to you when you were six, the sooner you will find peace in all of this. Believe me, it exists no matter how unbelievable it seems to you now and probably will for the next 10+ years.

The next four years are a blur, not to indicate that they were all dark years, but when you are older, you will realize that the next four years are some traumatizing ones. Moving through the years, you assume everything is normal. Everyone around you behaves as if it is normal. You will later learn that everyone in your life around this time were either oblivious or fearful. You experience life as we know it, as an African American girl growing up in an urban community. You experience some highs and you experience some lows. During these years you will also develop your motherly personality. You assume that life is supposed to be this way, but again, getting older will help you realize that this began the trend of your childhood being taken away from you. You start feeling "responsible" and "in charge" between the ages of six and ten. Being dropped at family members' houses, you witness things that shape you into believing that your life was provided for you to protect. This is a quality that will daunt you for years to come, but do not worry. You will recognize this trait of yours and learn how to turn it down.

One of the first things you remember during these years is being sat on a porch late night by your aunt because your mom refused her food stamps. You and your sibling visited this aunt's quite frequently and for years you will be oblivious to the fact that this aunt of yours does not operate under a sober mind. So when she allows you to stay out late, hang with boys twice your age, or for you to receive whippings for wetting the bed by your cousin who is only a few years older than you, you are not able to find the logic. You do not learn of her drug use until you are about 16 or 17 years old. Even then, you still assumed it was normal. Like the time you walked on the porch and witnessed someone in your family smoking out of a crack pipe and getting in trouble for witnessing it.

You will try so hard to make these images in your mind fake, you are going to put fire to your mind to erase whatever it is you think you saw during these years. So much to the extent that you will tell yourself you have never witnessed someone being beaten and stuffed in a trunk. You will try so hard to make these moments distant and false from your reality. But this is where you needed me. You needed me to tell you to address these traumatic events. Your coping skill of making it all "fake" will attempt to ruin you when it all comes back full speed. When you experience any uncomfortable moment in life, you will subject yourself to not only dealing with what's at hand, but all of these images plus more will plague over every issue you have going forward.

Now it is time to move. Life as you know it will be taking a full turn and you are relieved that your life is going to change. You will find deep comfort in thinking that you don't have to remember anything that happened while living in Chicago. The next year gives you hope. Everything appears to be going fine and from what you remember, there were no major traumatic events while living in this new place. It's just you, your mother, and your sibling at this time. Life feels like what one would call normal. I mean, if you grow up and forget to consider the time when you broke into someone's house with a group at 9 years old, or when you practiced Buddhism at this age without your mother's knowledge, or telling your mom about one account of being taken advantage of and not feeling that her reaction was appropriate. If you forget to consider these things, which you so often do, then it will appear that you had a normal year.

Chapter 2: It Isn't Normal

I want you to know that none of this is normal. The victimization, the traumatization, and the sights that you should have never seen. Growing up, you will witness others who have experienced similar things. You will find friends who relate to being molested, have seen loved ones do drugs, who knew what it felt like to be scared and displaying it in other ways. These friends will also have people in their lives who make all of this seem normal. It will become easy for you to downplay your experiences and to convince yourself that feeling sad or hurt was you being dramatic. However, you began to feel stressed and easily depressed by other things in life. You force the feelings of trauma onto outside situations in order not to think about the things that you were not supposed to discuss. Doing what any traumatized family structure does, you sweep it under the rug and at this point in your life, you have no plans to ever lift that rug. You know somewhere in your head, that lifting that rug would cost you people, things, and life as you know it. But you will eventually say to hell with those losses. I will be a part of your healing. While there's more under that rug that you are not necessarily ready to discuss, you need to shed light on the things that you are ready for. When you decide to, the rug should not be lifted until you are ready to face every dust mite under it.

Another part of healing will be learning how to release the blame. This is not all of your fault. You were not born into this world to create unforgiving childhood memories. You will spend many years taking blame for every "bad" thing that happened during these times. It will eventually drain you and you will attempt to leave life. You try to convince yourself many times, that if you were not here, none of these things would be happening. Thankfully, you will eventually learn, understand, and embrace the fact that most of these things were not in your control and the blame is not yours. Don't spend time trying to find out who the blame belongs to, but instead, ensure that you know it is not yours. You will learn that mental health issues are real and addiction is a sickness. For all of the things that you learn, there will be less fixation on who to let claim the blame. Letting go of the idea that the blame is yours and if not, then you must figure out who, takes you beyond the point of what you believe to be healing. Who is at fault for these chain of events is none of your concern.

While I cannot say at this time you have fully healed, I can say with 100% certainty that you are closer than you have ever been. As scary as it appears, you will have to face the fact of things like being molested, having family members with addictions, and witnessing many things that strip your innocence away from you. It will be scary to face it, but my hope is that reading this will help you build the strength in order to heal sooner. By healing sooner you may be able to avoid some of the pain. Even though this pain has made you into what you will become, you could do without more of it.

You are not alone, you will make it, and there is a way out even when it feels like there is not. This is a vital time to train your mind to fight when you start to feel like fighting is no longer an option. Even with the thought of taking your life, you know there are others like you. You know that other girls everywhere are mentally suffering with you, some even worse than you. In a way, this will help you keep going. It will inspire you to be different than most girls in your shoes probably would be. And when those around you take credit for what you did for yourself internally, your hate will grow stronger. This is where you will get eventually find yourself stuck. Amid being molested at six, nothing has driven you to the edge like the next chapter. And nothing will until you're about 23 years old. At 10 years old, life as it is known will be shaken up. The blurry year spent in Minnesota will come & go and the next chapter will be the hardest one yet. The eight years spent in Kalamazoo will feel like a lifetime and it will age you beyond reality. I do not mean this in a physical sense, but instead mentally.

You like starting over because you always imagine that the change will allow you to reinvent yourself. From small to big, starting over is a pleasing feeling at this point of your life. So on the road to Kalamazoo, Michigan you are filled with joy knowing that you will meet new family, new friends, and be in a new environment. Hope lives within you on your way there and for the first year that hope will be fulfilled. Your mom will become barely recognizable as you all get deeply involved into church. You will love this part of life because everything will seem as if it is good. This remains the case until a cousin you have not met, enters your life. Except he will not enter life as your cousin, but instead, your mom's boyfriend. You know your mom would never, so everything you hear family members saying you try very hard to make a lie. Until the lie can no longer be a lie.

Your mom will attempt to justify this situation at the point that she believes it is affecting you and your thoughts. She will explain to you that your 4th and 5th cousins do not really count as your cousins. It is at this point that you realize the lie is not a lie. Shortly after this, he will be practically living in the same house with you, your mom, and siblings. Following this, you will be teased in an argument by one of your cousins that your mom is a crackhead who dates her cousin. The part about dating her cousin will hurt you, you will not let go of this and for years it will cause you to have hate in your heart. You will learn later in life that the feeling of hating him is pain from embarrassment and it will hurt. It hurts at this point and at any other point of hearing people discuss your mom dating her cousin. You'll keep this from her most times to avoid her reaction, but keeping it all to yourself will twist the dagger. At this point finding an outlet would be ideal, but you may not have found a healthy one just yet.

As you go through the next few stages of life, your mental will get harder to control. You will become so unbelievably angry while still pretending that you are okay. You will learn how to pretend at great lengths to protect yourself from anything that may come with you appearing emotionally torn or weak. Up until middle school, I cannot recall exactly what happened, but an English teacher will see something in you that will change your entire life. And you may not feel it in that moment, but what she does is introduce you to writing in the form of pen paling. She will have concern due to your expression of dealing with stress at such a young age. In addition to writing, she will introduce you to the college ready program that will change your life even further and we will get there. You will not see it right now, in fact you will resist it right now, but these were the life changing moments for you. You will not be able to escape your reality just yet, but you are always closer than you have ever been before.

Chapter 3: Kalamazoo

02/20/2009 (2nd hour at school): "I don't know how I feel. I just want to be alone. But when I think about it again I don't want to be alone. I want to be surrounded by people. I hope my friends don't really take it to personal. I lashed out at 2 people one last night and one today! I hope I can control myself today and not get crazy on people, but I'm hoping that people can see just by the way I'm carrying on that I don't want to be bothered with! Well he's in my class right now, DP, and it's painful. I don't want to be around him right now. Not until I'm healed. Just hearing his name or glancing at him is painful. I don't even want to talk about him anymore. I just want to think and write. Well maybe writing about my thoughts my day will go better. I wish I could have a mood swing right now. It would be great if I can control these things. Then I don't think I would be as bad as I feel"

* * *

02/24/2009: "I don't know what it is..I don't think that I should go so many days without writing because it's hurting again. That same feeling is back in my heart! Ugh! It's really annoying when it just pops up and you don't know where it came from! Today Dannie broke my trust again. I know she's part of the reason it's coming back! I really miss J and thinking about him is making it even worst! I just don't want to look and be pathetic again! I can't breathe very well and tears are coming! God please help me! My only people that I am being strong for is my mom and brothers. Me and my mom's relationship has been great! Nothing bad! Me and my best friend J got into an argument! And this week is really not the best week. I have practice for the talent show, Central vs. Norrix game, and plans w/ friends. I just don't have the time and patience for this right now and that's what I like about being home because for some reason I can't get weak at home. It never shows when I'm around my mother and brothers and I love that but I can still feel it on the inside and it hurts bad! I need to talk to my English teacher Mrs. J. She can help it and so can my school counselor, Mrs. C. I need their help more than ever because I can crack any moment and I don't need this! J and Dannie the only two things that keep coming up and when they go down school and DP come up. There is no way I can't have anything on my mind but I need to find a way because I can't let my loved ones see me like that again. I hurt too many people during that time. I need a calming hobby. Today the only thing that crossed my mind when I felt like I was being stabbed was fighting. Why?? I don't know but I'm going to fix everything. It's a goal and I seem to accomplish goals most times, so yeah."

For as long as you have made sense of the world, you will forget about yourself. In the first entry that you still have access to, you make it clear that you are not being strong for yourself.

Nothing you do will be for yourself and this will eventually weigh on you. In addition to this, later in life you will learn that you cannot fix everything. You simply do not have the human ability to fix everything. As a 14 year old girl you adopted this mindset and hopefully by reading this you will not make it to 24 believing the same concept to be true.

* * *

03/04/2009 (At home on the couch): "Well I haven't wrote to myself in a while and I think that's a major problem! I'm hurting again but right now it's only on the inside and if I would have never stayed after school, outside would have been how my insides are feeling. I am pretty lost and I don't know what the cause but at this point idc. I want to have the shutdown because there's too many worries and I don't think I can hold them all in one hand! Maybe I do need counseling?! I want it but my mom won't approve, I know it. And it pisses me off to know that she can't approve of something that I think is best for me. I never write when I'm happy, that's probably the problem. I don't take note of it but I'm really hurting! Idk if it's worse but it hurts. I lashed out at Phabian today and it was because I was already burning and he added paper to the fire! Maybe I need to take Mrs. J's advice right now and help myself. Because right now I don't care who I hurt because people can't seem to see that they are hurting me every day! Until they actually, literally see it and that pisses me off even more! My head is pounding but writing is what I need the most right now! When I write I feel like I am telling someone my problems and they seem to have the perfect response even though I can't hear anything! When I was a little girl (smaller) I never pictured my life turning out like this, there's really nothing wrong with my life I just didn't picture it like this! But ugh I just got SUPER PISSED. I need to get my STUFF together now before I get older I wanna be better and I can make myself better and that's why I'm pissed! I just wanna break something now I need to stop thinking because trying to picture my future is pissing me off really FREAKING BAD before next school year I WILL be better. The people I hang with that's it. I need new friends because I kinda got a clue that that's whose causing all this. Those kids I call my friends I'm going to stop messing with anybody. I swear."

Part of this was normal teenage, middle school issues. Being upset about friends and relationships was not too far from abnormal at this age. However, in this writing there is something beyond middle school behavior. There is confusion on what is normal and what is not. There is confusion on how you even feel. Your emotions fluctuate as this is something that will become habit. In addition to this, your obsession with the future will start at this age. And even now, a decade later, one of your biggest pitfalls will be getting fixated on what the future will be like. This a very toxic trait that will obstruct in more ways than not for you.

* * *

03/08/2009 (Home sitting on the stairs): "I had a pretty good weekend. I didn't really do anything. Maray came over but I still had fun and I've been very happy! This was one of the best weekends in like a month. Me and my mom is fine, me and Mrs. J still pen paling! None of my friends have been pissing me off and every-

thing's been just right. The only thing that's getting me is my dad! I'm sick and tired of him lying to me and I strongly dislike that man but it's very hard to show on the outside. Well my life is going okay right now and I hope it continues."

* * *

04/19/2009 (Evening at home): "I was going to write to myself on April 15, 2009 but I forgot about it!! I am doing better, my life seems to be clearing just a little bit and it seems that God is pushing things outta my life and bringing in the better. I'm starting to realize what's important in life. My mom and I are doing perfectly fine but just a couple of days ago, I strongly disliked her! I guess my mom is pretty cool, but it seems she can't accept the fact that I'm 14! She's way too over reactive for the smallest reasons and she's ungrateful for me! She doesn't realize that I'm a perfect angel compared to other 14 year oldsz and she needs a wakeup call, it seems like sometimes she getsz it den at times she "think" she's got it, but idk! Well I feel pretty good about mahself!! Only itsz like I wanna be or should I say have a relationship with God. But somethings in dah way! I can't figure it out yet but I'll grab hold of it soon! And starting today 4-19-09, I'm, well I made 3 promises to myself...NO BOYz for at least a year! Bcuz that's problems. I don't need a boy in mah life!! And going to church today made me realize that the most important things are life and education!! Well I've lost a couple friends but that's actually a good thing. We're not beefing, we just separated and dats even better! I love myself right now but it seems like either something is wrong or something is missing! Idk why but I trust God to let meh know!

P.S. Life is very confusing!"

* * *

05/16/2009 (Just got home from T's): "Ugh. My mother disgusts meh! She say I'll find anything to pick a fight with my cousin but that B*TCH will find anything to defend that bastard!! He's not changed and he never will. He's doing the same sh*t as before and I give it a couple months before he punches her stupid a** again!! At times I don't even look at her as a woman. She's just a sorry excuse for a single mother! She makes all the real single moms out here look bad! She is outrageous to me!! Can't say one thing about him without her defending him! Like he's not her cousin! Gurl please! The other day she told meh she'd stab meh! WTF is she serious. That only showed me that she truly doesn't love me! She's only taking care of me because I'm her daughter! She always saying f*ck me...calling me b*tches when she gets madd & she needs tah cut all that out becuz I've had thoughts! Deep thoughts! Thoughts that could put me away for some time! I wish she could be normal, like a regular mom!!! Nd I hope she knows I'm not stupid, I know she's on powder! Nd She's a flippin weed head! I pray that god will make that woman better some day! Just some day! Other than her, my life is perfectly fine."

Wow. This entry hurts you. It hurts you because its hard to recognize the girl in this entry and so many versions to follow. At the point of revisiting this entry you will not believe these words you wrote. It will bring a sense of peace knowing that you will not remain in this state of mind forever. You will grow to a point of not being able to imagine speaking of your mother so ill. This is hurt. You will be hurt and you have every right to be, but these words you speak will come from a dark and corrupted place. Feel this anger, but do not act upon it. For it is only a temporary feeling. At the time it will feel what you imagine hell to be like, but healing from this space will be so rewarding.

* * *

06/17/2009 (In the bed): "Ugh! I'm so pissed...Still in this motherf*cking house about to commit suicide because I've been in this hell hole way too f*cking long! I'm so fricking bored and just disgusted. I've been in the house since the summer started babysitting these damn kids. Who in the hell wants to be here. When she finally was about to let me go she doesn't because I lied and said I talked to someone. F*cking Dipshit! That's the dumbest lie ever to get mad about. I just said I talked to Bee when I really didn't. So what the f*ck are you mad about. She is the dumbest mom ever. I f*cking hate her. She gets mad over nothing! Maybe if she didn't have a f*cked up temper I would have never lied and we wouldn't be having this problem. But no, she gets mad at stupid sh*t! And she embarrassed me for no f*cking reason in front of a group of teenage girls who probably laughed their a**es off at me. I don't even wanna go anywhere for the whole summer. She's so stupid I can't stand her! I'm staying in my room forever. She is a stupid b*tch!"

Wow, again. There is so much hurt and anger in this entry towards your mom. I only say wow because it is so hard to imagine that you had such animosity towards someone who you have grown a strong relationship with. I am sure at the time of writing this entry you will not see the lessons in all that is going on. As cliché as it may sound, there is purpose in all pain. Do not find your self so hooked on the emotion that you are unable to find healthier ways to cope with the things that are bothering you.

* * *

06/30/2009 (In bed; Just woke up): "Well it's been a while! My life has been awright I guess?! Me and my mom is perfectly fine! We've been getting along more than we have my whole life! I hate to say it but depression gives my mom the best attitude! She's very depressed right now and has been for a while. Our lights has been shut off and they're illegally turned back on. Our cable is off, rent was just past due but we've been paying that off! This is the most she's ever talked to me, but she also has downfalls. She's not being as strong as she can be! She sleeps too much and she doesn't have to. She's also taking pills and smoking way too much! She forgets things too much and that needs to stop! I'm doing good behind all of that. No boyfriend, no problems! Not currently talking to anyone but I do like this guy named SJ. He has a girlfriend though. Well no drama lately except for with CS. Ugh, she's disgust! But other than that I'm loving Summer 09'! bby!"

I am so sorry. I am sorry that at such a young age you know about everything your family is going through. This is a lot for you. I wish I could show you why all of this is essential to who you will become. However, you are strong. You know that there is something greater and that is why you push pass all of this. This entry is scary because you have not only noticed the burden of the cable, lights, rent, and so much more, but you constantly refer to these issues as "ours" and "we." This shows how much of the adult role you have taken on, at only 14 years old. You are able to identify that your mom is suffering from depression and that she is self-medicating. This is probably one of the most touching entries because it is a clear depiction of just how early you were afforded less childhood protections than the average.

* * *

08/02/2009 (Bedroom floor): "I f*cking hate my mom. She is sooo f*cking stupid! She isn't a real mom. At all. She's a stupid B*TCH! Ugh...I'm so pissed that I can destroy this f*cking house and run away. I wish I had money because I would leave right f*cking now! I swear! I'm so f*cking tired of being in this house I haven't stayed the night on my choice of day over any of my friends house in about a year. In this whole year I only stayed the night at Nae's and only when my mom offers! I don't have a mom or a grandmother. She put me on punishment because I forgot to find a shoe! What the f*ck! I have no choice but to forget when she gives me a million things to do in one minute. And I know she's showing off for her cousin who she's sleeping with (nasty b*tch)! Her attitude changes every time she's around him! She makes me so mad that if she died right now at this point I wouldn't give a f*ck! On my baby brother, I won't even go to her funeral. I hate that b*tch. I truly do. Why did she have to be my mom. I wish I could switch with my friends because she's so stupid. UGH! I'm so mad, STUPID F*CK-ING B*TCH! SN: I am currently talking to Deezy, Josh likes me. I am loving my friends, but hating my life because of my wanna be mother."

Crazy that this entry came just a month after you writing that you and your mom were doing the best that you had ever been doing. I believe the fluctuations are what made your hate and anger so strong. Being so young, it will confuse you, which ultimately creates fear. The fear that you hold will come out in other ways. Another heart breaking entry, along with many more to follow. It breaks my heart, because you needed me. You needed me before I even realized who "me" is. Although I am extremely thankful for the progress you and your mom will make, it still saddens me that I was not there for you during a time where anger was leading your life.

* * *

08/09/2009 (In my room on the floor): "Once again I have to stay in the f*cking house! Ugh she is sooo nerve wrecking! I had to stay in with this dumb a** family for the whole weekend! Friday, Saturday, and Sunday! I hate that b*tch. I wish she just dies and burn in hell! I had to stay in for telling her she doesn't know anyone in my program and for staying in my room. What the f*ck! If I have an attitude why would I sit in her face with it so I can get in more trouble. I'm 14 motherf*cking years old! What does she expect! Dumb a** b*tch! I'm always in the house, this s*it is ridiculous! I'm running the f*ck away tomorrow. I swear. I can't do this sh*t anymore. UGH!! I'm so f*cking upset! Sh*t Sh*t Sh*t! I feel like breaking something. UGH AHHHHH! I just wanna kill myself right f*cking now!!! I'm not watching her f*ck face kids or nothing...I hate her! I just wish she just died right now. I'm tired of this house. I been in the house for too long. She think just because she let me go a couple places that would do it, NO! Compared to *my friends I don't do sh*t! She's a single, miserable, dipsh*t. I hate her!"*

I wish you would acknowledge the deeper issues related to your anger. Deeper issues meaning, Man and the drugs. That has to be why you're so angry, right? At 14 you began having your first suicidal thoughts. These thoughts came from a deeper place than just being forced to stay in the house. Speaking of your siblings who mean the world to you, in such ways is also a clear sign that this was deeper than staying in the house. You are not wishing death upon your own mother due to a punishment. Explore why you have so much hate in your heart in order to clear some of it sooner rather than later.

* * *

08/18/2009 (In my room @ 2:00am): "I'm running away tomorrow. I can't take it. Yesterday I got so mad I almost struck back at her. I have to get out for somedays...I can't take her...She woke up with an attitude and wants someone to worship the ground she walks on. LIKE HELL! So she doesn't understand that I'm a 14 year old girl! She tripped over shorts! Every girl my age wears them. I'm fast because I wear shorts! Well in that case every girl in the world is fast. She is too overreactive and I can't take it anymore! I'll be back and when I do I'll hit you up. Byeeee! Love you journal, you help a lot!"

Journaling helped you get through the darkest moments of your life. Referring to "hitting the journal up," shows how much trust you had in this part of your life, as if it were the only person you had. Ironic that it will end up turning into a dream to share, what you consider a powerful tool.

* * *

09/06/2009 (In my bed): "I haven't wrote to you since the day before I ran away. I ran away for hours then my mom found me...I had planned to stay away for two weeks but she looked for me...ugh, me and that lady who calls herself my mother has been on and off. Nothing has really changed. She gets on my last f*cking nerves still! The only reason I don't want to move is because of Duck...I do because my mom is so f*cking stupid! She got fired and it's her f*cking fault. I'm happy she did but she acts like she still doesn't care! She's still not trying to change her ways...so I'm not changing mine...She's still smoking cigarettes, weed, I believe doing powder, drinking, and sleeping with her cousin! Man life is a B*TCH! I don't even know what to say. I'm so confused about everything right now. I just want school to start so I won't have to be in this hell hole. UGH!"

So lost...At this age you are so lost and broken. And again, I am sorry. I am sorry that I show up so much later, but you will get through this. You may not believe it yet, but you handled a lot at 14, you knew too much at 14. It took away from your innocence, it created anger, and it will leave a mark. But, please just trust the process.

* * *

12/16/2009: "Seems like forever! I know I haven't wrote to you in forever! I miss you so much. I have sooo much stuff to tell you.

Well first off me and my favorite cousin Dee fell out. I betrayed her. I told her business to one of our other cousins and I really don't feel bad, but it's still kinda sad because she trusted me with her whole life. I miss her soo much though. & I miss her stories, but hey, that's how the world is and I've learned to face it and deal with it! Right now at this moment in time I'm f*cking horrible. I am in my room on the floor crying my eyes out! I don't know what the f*ck to do!! I f*cking hate people. I just got my number changed. I wish I could just f*cking stay locked in my room for 3 more years and then magically become rich, but I know I have to work these three years if change is what I want. Next year I'm moving to Atlanta, Georgia and I can't f*cking wait! I hate it here. Living in Kalamazoo has been the worst time of my life!! I f*cking hate it. I hate it. I hate it!! I go to a new school, Portage Northern! I'm not accepted there at all and I hate it. I pretend because I'm getting a great education and I know I'm gonna have a better future there than being at Kalamazoo Central, where I skipped school four times a week!! It's just that I was so accepted at central and it's not like I'm a lame at Portage, but I'm lonely as hell!! I'm the NEW GIRL! I hate being new. But I can't change it, well anyways I'm about to be 15 at the end of the month, but I don't even give a f*ck! I hit the breaking point and I'm soo sad. I've had great days since the last time I wrote you, like amazing days but I've also had the worst days of my life. Friends are fake. I f*cking hate when people say they're my friend because they're all the same phony fake dumb a** liars! I'm tired of people's bullsh*t. I'm tired of trying to impress everyone! I'm just so damn tired!! I don't member if I let you in but my mom finally got CPS called on her, but they ain't do sh*t cuz I ain't tell them sh*t! I was about to move to Chicago. We got into a lot of huge fights *and a lotta sh*t happened but that kind of woke her up. She starting to let me live but sh*t she still ain't that cool. Boys, sh*t. I wish I can murder every man that ever hurt me, including my dad! I f*cking hate men. What the fuck are they here for? Why?! WTF! I feel so alone right now! I have nobody's shoulder to cry on! So lonely I don't know what to do. School used to be my cover up but now that I go to portage it's causing more stress. I just wish one man and one woman could pop up in my life magically and I'll live with them. I mean a man and a woman who is just true, sincere, trustworthy, respectful, just two people. My life is so f*cking f*cked that two days ago I would walked right through a gun fight and stood there. The bad is beating the good in my life! On November 21, 2009 at 2:00am I lost my virginity to Deezy. I love him, I honestly do, but I don't think he was the one & if he is, that's real magic. There is no way in hell he cares as much as I do. It seems like it, but that's because I'm not a sucka & I don't let nobody see my feelings! I just don't know what to do! I need Jesus! Duck, the last boy I wrote you about, broke my f*cking heart which is nothing new. Hurted, but f*ck it. I need to suck it up and get used to reality, right? I love my mom more than I did two months ago. She ain't perfect, but she's better & that's all that matters. Ughh...I've got into it with so many people, met so many people, since the last time I wrote to you!! You done missed out on a lot, but I'll keep you posted. P.S. I'm raising two little boys, Kam'rom and Kaleb. No matter what she says I'm raising these children and she's just someone that makes sure they're okay after me!!"*

One of the hardest entries because it shows so much trauma, hurt, and loneliness. At 14 years old, you have lost your virginity, you're skipping school, pretending to be happy, and referring to the desire to die as if it is an activity. To keep telling you to stay strong and that you will get through this, feels unrealistic to me sometimes and I know for a fact that you will get through it. This is all tough, it's something you will learn to suppress in order to please those around you, but the freedom will come when you no longer have that desire to impress or please others. You note in this entry that you do not let people see your feelings. Carrying this value of not letting your emotions play out will hurt you more than it protects you. This is your truth, your story, it is what makes you. Maybe by the end of this I will have the right words to say to you in order for you to push through it all with minimal pain. However, at this time, I cannot seem to find those words because I feel that pain. I know it is not an easy thing to escape or to see a brighter side of it. Just hang tight. That feeling you have felt about being "different" or "special" will eventually make sense. You will see that there is purpose in all of this pain you have felt.

* * *

12/17/2009: "Hello, I feel so much better! But why does feeling better always feel lonely! Like when I went to Portage Northern?! I feel that I'm doing better there but I'm lonely & I got my number changed & deleted some of the old peoples. I feel better I haven't had any, any, any drama today. But I also feel lonely because no one really has the new number and I'm getting no calls. Shonnie and Dannie cheered me up. I feel weird though. I don't know what the feeling is or where it came from. I wish I was closer to GOD! Because last night when I broke down to him, I heard him speak to me, "Everything is gonna be ok my child." It's like we were having a conversation, I really love Jesus a lot. Anyhow, things aren't going so great with me and Deezy. I think my ex-bestfriend since yesterday likes him! They're too close, but I can find a way to live without them. I have a f*ck everybody attitude right now. I can count on one hand how many people I actually give a sh*t about right now! Two days ago I woulda been able to go on for days, but I guess I realized who is there for me and always will be. I guess I see who real & who's fake. I'm so thankful God finally opened up my eyes and made me see clearly."

* * *

12/18/2009 (Just got home): "Once again she pissed me off. This dumb a** girl got mad because I deleted one of her boyfriend's number out of my phone. I repeat MY phone. WTF. It's not hers. She has her own f*cking phone so she slapped me for something that happened two days ago and she didn't do anything when it happened. I really don't like my mom. Other than her, I'm loving life. I love Shonnie & Dannie! My f*cking all-time best friends. I guess me and Nae are doing good. Me and Deezy ain't talked in three days. I got my number changed & the bastard ain't getting it! He makes me sick too! He's really a f*cking liar. Men are stupid & I hate them too! I guess life is cool. Still can't wait to grow up & never see my mom again. I can move whenever I want, but right now is not the time for me! So yeah, I'm still in that f*ck friends mood, but I'm cool so bye.

P.S. Me & my auntie are perfect. We apologized to each other & I love her to death. My grandmother is cool, we doing ohkay I *guess. My aunt D...well I ain't talked to her, but we back cool or whatever."*

* * *

12/24/2009 (11:18am): "Ohkay so I thought about somethings today...I write to you & tell you all my business & you know me, but you don't KNOW me. If you know what I mean. Like you know a lot about my personal life & stuff but you don't know about me! So I'm gonna write a summary about me. I'm 14 years old, in 17 days I'll be 15. I was born in Chicago & moved to Minnesota when I was one then when I was two, I moved back to Chicago until I was nine. When I turned nine I moved back to Minnesota then at 10, I moved to Michigan. I just found out that on February 1, 2010 I'm moving to Atlanta, GA! Which I am so excited for! I really don't like Kalamazoo. It's so boring! & the people! Don't even get me started on them! Anyways I love spending time with my family, watching movies, music, TV, hanging out, fast food, being cute, shopping, and a host of other things. I love my 3 brothers to death & I'd kill for them! School IS cool & I love getting an education, but I hate waking up so early! Sometimes school is boring though. I love Golden Girls, Bad Girls Club, & Phineas & Ferb, best shows! When I grow up I wanna be either a Social Worker or Senior Advertising Executive! Friends are foes, nobody is real and I trust no one but God! My hair is the most important thing to me & that's real! I fights for my hair! I hate looking a mess. I dig in my nose a lot and I don't care who in the hell is looking! I hate when girls talk sh*t. I love fighting, but I don't do it often anymore. I love Myspace and Facebook. I hate Burger King, McDonalds is the place to be! I wanna be married by 32. I want one or two kids & I *wanna adopt. I'm proud to be who I am! I'm sometimes conceited & that's just me, I can't help it. I keep a couple close ones but most of everybody are fake! I've pulled a couple fake moves, I'm not 100% real, but I know how far to take it. I've made plenty mistakes, but yet I don't regret anything because everything that happened yesterday happened so that everything that happens today could happen! That's my motto. I really don't care what other people think about me because no one that is not important matters to me. I go by Imani Monet, Monet, or Mani. It doesn't matter as long as you know me. & that's pretty much it.*

P.S. Me & my mom are doing fantastic. Chicago on Saturday and everything's all good."

10 years later and all I can say is, wow.

* * *

01/03/2010: "It's a new year! I just got home from Chicago & I feel great!! I love my life 100% there is really nothing bothering me right now. I'm 15 years old and my birthday was three days ago. I spent a week in Chicago! My dad is great..my stepmother is ohkay & everything is just awesome right now. Me & my mom are doing better than ever! I love her so much & we've been bonding! A LOT! My brothers are still my life & I love them. Not really caring about friends & I'm just happy school starts tomorrow! UGH I'm so not ready to go back. Me & my mom, I just can't get off of the fact that we're just so close right now! I love her! I ask God to forgive me for my past with my mom! Atlanta here I come February 1st! I'm just so excited."

* * *

01/21/2010: "*I haven't wrote in a long time! My life has been one crazy kick a** roller-coaster! Why don't I just start off with friends?! So Nae grandparents tried to pull us apart! WHY?! I don't know!! It's crazy how you could be that old and jealous of two high school cousins relationship! As long as I live I have nothing else to say to them or her mother who doesn't even have custody of her! They asked if we were gay. Like seriously, be forreal, if I was gay...MY COUSIN!?! Would be the last girl I look at. They really have some nerve! But I'll just pray about it & get over it. Bee, we're still friends but we don't hang as much. Shonnie is my best friend, I love her. She's always here for me & when I move I'll miss her the most! I really don't talk to other people anymore. Zhanaria & Kelsie are really cool & I hang out with them every day! I have associates, but I try to stay more to myself now & I find that works better. I don't need extra people in my life. Family! Why don't I talk about that. My brothers are still my life & I pray almost every chance I get that my brothers grow up to be SOMEBODY! I hope they're not failures because of the environment they're in. I miss my Chicago family. Visiting made me wanna be around them all the time! I feel like I can be myself around them without being judged! I love those crazy people. Me & my dad are pretty closer than any other time. I love him and I don't think I could live without him. He's not the perfect father, but he's good enough and he tries. My mom and I are pretty close. We have major up and downs, but we're really closer than ever. She's cool even though she doesn't have it all. I need to work on stop wishing horrible things on her when she pisses me off because I do love her. My mom is back talking* *to her sisters and her mother. So family is really great right now! Boys, aha. It's going pretty good. I have a boyfriend and his name is Anthony. He's cool and he really likes me! I talk to other guys but I'm not that into any of them, they're just cool people. I've talked to Deezy and I know he wants me back, but I'm learning from mistakes and I refuse to go back down that road. I mean he does love me and I'm not saying that because I know boys who said it and didn't really mean it. When Deezy says it, I'm almost positive he means it but I'm just not into him like I used to be which is honestly sad. Boys are crazy, but hey! I can't live with them, can't live without them! School is cool! I enjoy being at Portage Northern! It's cool and a way better learning environment for me. I like it and I like the people there. I mean I'm motivated to learn and it's just great! I still hate waking up early, but as I get into the day I actually enjoy being in school. Life is pretty much good right about now! I have problems everyday like any other teen, but I'm cool. I'm not stressed about anything. I'm almost always positive now and I feel so great about myself and my life! I'm reading a book called The Most Important Decisions You'll Make by Sean Covey and I really like this book. I just started yesterday, it's a really good book! It's turned on a lot of bulbs in my head in only one day so I can't wait to get through the rest of it. It just gets me motivated to be the best I can be and keeps me thinking strictly positive! I'm so focused on my future right now and I really hope I get to experience going to Spelman College. That's my dream for now and exams are NEXT WEEK, OMG! I know! But I'm pretty ready to take them. I'm so ready, I'm learning good study habits and I'm doing good. I have so much confidence in myself and I'm totally loving it!"*

* * *

01/22/2010: "Oh my god! I don't understand how someone can be the happiest person in the world then only 24 hours later the saddest, most hurt person in the world! I don't understand life! I wish everyone could just personally have real conversations with GOD. Because I need him to guide me forreal. Maybe he's testing me or maybe I thought I was happy and really I just wasn't, idk what it is!!! I'm just fed up with my life itself right now! I did really good coping today. My mom pissed me off soooooooooo freaking bad and I didn't wish or say any harsh things on her! I did the best because usually I would've wished so many terrible things on her. I thank God for life but it's just all so crazy right now and I don't need this by exams! GOD HELP ME! And I'm praying every chance I get

P.S. My mom go mad because Bee sent me a picture of people having sex?! Now what control did I have over that.

P.S.A Today I told Shonnie that when I die I want my journal to be a book or at least before I die! But nobody could read it before it's published!"

* * *

01/23/2010: "Why is she doing this to me? She is making my life a living hell! And she's doing it on purpose! Okay so first Nae can't hang out with me and her grandparents hate me, then she tells my dad all these lies and he's mad at me, then Shonnie's mom thinks I'm a horrible person and she doesn't want her daughter to have anything to do with me! I just don't understand why this is happening to me! Everyone just thinks I'm this horrible outrageous teenager, when I'm really a DAMN GOOD teenager! I have prob-

lems like any other, but I just so happen to be the worst one! I do everything I can and I'm not appreciated at all. I'm a 15 year old African American girl who was born and partially raised in Chicago and I'm GOOD! What the fuck! I mean I go to school, I wanna make something of my life, I take care of my brothers every day and I still maintain good grades as a freshmen in high school. I don't have the greatest relationship with my mom but I still do what the f*ck I gotta do and it just doesn't count for anything! The devil is trying his hardest to bring me down and I need God because the devil is doing a good a** job and bringing me down. I do too much to be in this condition. I TRY! And that doesn't mean anything."

You cannot recognize at this point that you are feeling lonely. You are feeling like the world is against you, when all you try to put out is positive energy. At this age, it is hard to see that you are everything that you are supposed to be. You will take all the misunderstandings of others and hang onto it. Allowing this to drain and discourage you. At this point it would probably do you well to seek additional resources for help with the transformation of your mental health over the next year. It is apparent that this is the point that you began to suffer from the life that you were afforded upon birth. I know it feels tough right now, and just telling you to hang in there may seem so cliché that you don't even almost hold on to the thought. I wish we were at a point where I have the right words to help you, but truth be told, I am not yet there. I cannot tell you how to cope with this feeling when this is something we continue to struggle with. The only thing I can assure you, is that there will be many more situations to help us learn to stay afloat. Hold on to that thought that you will eventually get there, please.

* * *

02/11/2010: "Ohkay here I go, life is pretty good right now. You missed out on a couple things but I'm still letting them out because they're still kinda bothering me. Okay, 1ˢᵗ Shonnie's mom! Oh my. She popped my bubble, lol. She pissed me off to the maximum! I guess she doesn't want me and Shonnie together anymore which I don't give a f*ck about, but it bothered me because she didn't have a reason to. She doesn't want us together because of the sh*t with me and my mom. I'm "influencing" her daughter when Shonnie is 14 muthaf*cking years old and she know what she do and why. So yeah, and it also pissed me off because I'm sick of people trynna judge me and don't know sh*t about me. It hurt me soo bad because she just added to everybody else who don't know sh*t about me! They don't know that I work my f*cking a** off not to be a failure or how much and how long I been taking care of my brothers, they don't know that I've thought about killing myself and dealt with that sh*t by myself!! With no f*cking help at all! They don't know that I was molested at age six! Do they? NO! and that sh*t pisses me off cuz don't nobody know sh*t and always wanna judge me like I'm this horrible a** person. That's why I don't rely or depend on no f*cking body! Forreal. Next subject, my house hold itself is doing great. I don't think we moving anymore cuz my momma wanna stay in this lame a** town. Why? IDK!!! But oh my God! About two days ago it hit me. I really wasn't bothered by the fact that Deezy is in love with somebody else and we weren't on speaking terms but last week it hit me harder than ever before! I can't help *but think about him and how much I need that man. I feel like I gave him a lot and I did a lot for him! I lied to my mom about him, traded on any of my friends for him, I gave him my pride, the most valuable thing I owned and I feel like he didn't appreciate me! And he's just so important to me. I don't know how I let him go and get away from me, the sh*t is really killing me on the inside and even though Anthony makes me very happy and I really like him, Deezy still left an empty hole that Anthony can't fill in! I just never thought it'd end up like this. I never thought I'd feel like this about Deezy but I feel like he used me and I can't believe how quick he fell in love with this new girl! It hurt so f*cking bad because he left me without warning and I feel like I can't cry because my tears will mean nothing and Anthony is my boyfriend for a month today. We started talking 4 months ago, so yeahh, prolly longer than that and I like him a lot, that's why I don't understand what's happening. Nobody in this world can tell me I don't love the hell outta Deezy. I love that man to death and I just can't believe how he acts towards me. I honestly wish I could be happy for him and his new girl, but there's no way, I can't. I try my hardest to give my all to Anthony to get over it, but EVERYDAY! There's something there to remind me of us! And I can't help but blame myself for us because I played around and he really wanted to be with me, but I wasn't ready. I wouldn't leave Anthony for him because I know that chance is gonna come and I can't keep doing that to myself. I do wanna see Deezy though. I haven't seen him since the middle of December and I just gotta see him, but whatever! There's that, finally got that outta my head, but yeah life is great other than that, I'm very happy."*

* * *

02/16/2010: "Ohkay, I've hit the breaking point! I f*cking love Deezy and I can't get over it. I don't know why he's doing this to me. I mean I really don't. I can tell myself all day every day that I don't care about that boy, but I have never had this feeling for anyone no matter how much I thought I liked someone. I've come to realize that no one in this world today can take his place and I f*cking hate that I feel that way. I really do. I try to make myself be happy for him and his new girl but I can't do it. I wanna f*cking kill her like seriously. They got tattoos with each other name and I half way died when I heard that. I can't believe that he could live without me because I can't do this sh*t! It worked for a minute, but idk. I would honestly do anything! To get him back. Everyday I'm reminded of something and it's like I lose oxygen or something idk but it's hard to do this without him and then I really feel like he used me and I let him. I can't even say if I believed him every time he said he loved me because I felt and still somewhat feel that he meant it but I just don't know. And he told me he couldn't live without me. I wonder if he meant it because it seems like he's doing perfect without me and it seems like he doesn't want me back. I really like Anthony but I have a feeling that I'm gonna hurt him because of how much I love Deezy. And that's the last thing I want to happen. It's kind of already happening, but idk. I can't believe how much Deezy likes his new girl. This the only boy I've ever been willing to fight for!! Never even wanted to fight for J and that was my boy! But Deezy is just, I don't even know the word. I just love him and I wish I can go back in time to tell him that and do all I didn't. He said I'm not ready to be in a serious relationship and I

*wasn't and I still don't know if I am, but I just know I can't live w/
o him whether I wanna play or be serious. I just can't function w/
o him and I feel like he's dedicating his life to this new girl and he
shouldn't be! But hey idk whatever ends up happening I guess it'll
be for a "good" reason. So yeahh. God does everything for a specific
reason. I just don't understand this one I guess."*

When you come back to read the last couple entries, it will be
very disturbing to you to see that you were so far in lust at 15.
So many young girls in this same position with no one to talk to
and direct them that there is life outside of attention and accep-
tance of a man. It may be healthy to start seeking a therapist at
this point, but you are so consumed in trying to fix and control
things that you are distracted from the main issue at hand. The
anger that will structure and lead your character is being built
during these times. Reach out to those who you identify as a support and start the conversation surrounding something like therapy. You have been raised to believe that therapists and mental
health are things that do not pertain to you, but it is evident that
they do. At 15 you believe you are in love and it may surely feel
like love, but you have no idea. You will look back at this and almost find it comical. Try not to get so hooked on people and situations, because it too will serve as a weakness for you. It will set
you up to enter adulthood this way and make for situations being so much harder than they have to be. All the things that you
are looking for other people to accept or love about you, try accepting and loving it yourself first.

* * *

02/17/2010: "*Life really sucks...*"

* * *

02/25/2010: "*Well hey there. Haven't wrote in a minute and a lot of things has happened.*"

* * *

03/01/2010: "*I started writing a couple days ago but I got caught up and didn't have time to finish...I am so ready to get out of school. I'm so ready for summer. School is so boring! But wow...ohkay, I talked to Deezy and I told him how I felt and I thought it went pretty good and I went to his house and we almost had sex but I came on my period and I'm kinda glad I did...then after that I heard that when we did it he had an STD, which turned out to be a lie, and when I found out I wanted to f*cking kill him!! It turned out not be true so I'm better now but anyhow the day after I found out about whatever he came over and we didn't speak. We got into a small argument and that was that. We haven't said anything to each other and I really don't care. The only thing is that I CANNOT get bored because I can only think about him and it's really stressful...I don't even wanna go off into that and I currently don't talk to ANYONE; solo dolo is how I am. I just don't have time right now. Other than that whole lil situation I'm doing perfectly fine. Me and my mom have formed a relationship and I really love it. I thought a lot and my mom has had a very rough life and I'm starting to understand why she is the way she is and I really love my mother a lot! Anyhow it's about that time of the school year and I'm soooo ready for summer 10'. I'm bored w/ school but that's it I guess.*"

It will become clear how important you and your mom's relationship actually is to you. It will hurt you that it gets worse after this point and that it will be so up and down. Her mental illness and your inability to cope will present itself strongly within the relationship. Try finding ways to better cope in order to avoid more pain. It may feel easier to cope in unhealthy ways like fighting, being angry, having attachment issues, and more, but don't value the "easiness" of these situations. As long as you remember that healing is the end goal, then it will become easier overall to deal with all of the things life will throw at you.

* * *

03/15/2010: "Oh my...soooo much little crazy stuff has happened in the last 14 days. Crazy world...so lemme start off w/ family. I love my fams, my brothers are still my world! My mom and I are really honestly truly doing better than ever in 15 years! Like seriously, I love her and I feel like I don't have to lie to her and I can be open with her. She is really a good person and I regret any and everything I've ever done behind her back! I'm not putting anyone before her although my brothers are my 1ˢᵗ priorities. My friends are cool right now. I guess me and Bee are really close and she is my bestie through everything we've been through. Nae's grandparents are getting over themselves. I went over her house Saturday and I did talk to them even though I promised myself I wasn't. They're okay and me and Nae are starting to get back to where we were in our friendship. Me and Shonnie starting to talk slowly but that's really it on the friend tip because I really don't f*ck with too many people...Anyhow, you know what's next, the guys. Ohkay well first off I don't f*ck with Deezy. He's a f*ck boy and I don't like him. He think he on cuz he got flunkies following after him, but Deezy is really a flunky himself. Sooo...yea. But ugh, we got into it because he tried to stunt on me but I don't even give a f*ck! I think I'm really done with Anthony this time. We had started back talking, but he's just too f*cking rude and I don't have time for him and his anger problems. Anyhow life is good right now, could be better but it's cool...I've been thinking a lot and I really do wanna be saved and I wanna be really close with God! I really do! And something's holding me back and I need some help with it. I know this is what I want because I've thought about it so much. I'm like a 100% sure. I'm tired of not living the right way because things always go wrong when you don't live right...oh and I smoked weed for the first time. It was really stupid but I wanted to know why my mom is addicted to it and weed is stupid! I don't even understand how people smoke it as a hobby because it's just stupid. It's definitely not for me! Well I filled you in with most of everything that's been going on! Life is cool and I'm good sooo...I'm loving it right now!"

* * *

03/25/2010: "When I die I wanna be known...but I wanna go to heaven...

Ohkay, I don't know why I feel the need, but today I wanna go a little deeper. Starting from when I was young. I'm gonna write about alllllllll the things I can't get off of my mind and bothers me every day. Ohkay...when I was younger I hated my dad. I love him now and I thank him for everything he has done but when I was younger I had hate for him. I could never understand or put it together on why he didn't love me. I just was very confused and I just *didn't like him. We didn't ever talk and when we did it was very awkward. I love him now. We're not perfect daughter and dad but we're better. That still bothers me a lot and affects me because when he doesn't answer the phone now I think he's avoiding me or walking out. I think about it on most days. That did a lot in my life. I am so against dead beat dads. I hate men who don't take care of responsibility because of how my dad was when I was younger. I don't recall my relationship with him getting better until I was about 10. And it wasn't permanent then. My mom was never around. I saw her, but not enough. My auntie Laine basically raised me and my brother Keanan. I forgave my mom for choosing the streets, but I'll never forget. Everything I'm writing today nobody that's alive today knows about most of, nobody knows my take on the whole life thing, but anyhow family is really important to me and I love my family. When I grow up I do wanna be involved with them, but not my mom. I really don't want be that close with her because of how much pain she has caused, but idk. When I was about six years old, one day my mom went out with her friends and one of her friend's son watched me and Keanan. I think he was about 12 or 13 and I was sleep and I woke up to him touching me in a place that he shouldn't have touched. He kept asking if it felt good and telling me to shush. And right now to this day I blame my mom! If she wouldn't have been a street junkie and stayed w/ me and Keanan it wouldn't have happened. I wish that I can rewind time and undo it but I can't and I told my mom one time what happened and she "for fake" tried to do something about it but she really didn't care and for that I will never ever ever tell anyone else what happened. If she didn't care about me being molested, who would. NOBODY! I try not to think about it and I try to block it* out and forget but that's not gonna happen. I think about it at least 3 times a week depending on what kind of week I have. It's crazy how it happened and every time I saw him I would act normal because I felt like if I told anybody or acted different I would have to go to court and I really did not wanna do that. Another thing that really gets to me is how my mom did or is doing powder. She's basically a f*cking crackhead and that really destroys me on the inside and it's just a horrible topic for me. I don't wanna get too deep but that sh*t kills my insides forreal! So I'm not gonna go into it too much. I don't regret losing my virginity at 15. I still stand by my decision today and I don't care how anyone looks at the situation. I look at my auntie like she's my biological mother. I really love her and I'd die for her. *Rest of entry ripped out*

P.s. I also am very bothered by the fact that my mom puts men before her children. She lets her problems come between her and her children. And how she hasn't done anything for me since I was in the 8th grade and I'm almost at the end of my 9th grade year! It's just crazy to me, but oh well."

* * *

04/06/2010: "School just started back and it's pretty cool. I'm happy to be back. School is like my escape from life. For spring break I went on a college tour in Atlanta, GA. I had a lot of fun and somewhere along the line I started liking RD. I don't know if it's a serious like right now but I do like him. Anyhow I am very upset right now and I can honestly blow up into pieces. Okay, I love my mom, I truly do but I've never seen her like this. She is wayyyy too dependent. I like do not understand what is really motivating her not to get a job when she has four kids?! She can't possibly be *happy w/ the life she's living with no job! I'm not happy at all and I'm beginning to think that she can't take care of us. She doesn't do ANYTHING, but sleep and eat all day!! How could you possibly be happy with that knowing that you can't do for your kids. She is so dependent on the man she is w/ and he doesn't do anything! We're always broke and she doesn't have a car. She's scared to ask him for rides and it's really getting under my skin! I just don't understand! I'm way more independent than her and it's sad. She's sooo f*cking lazy and it's just horrible and I wanna tell her how I feel, but it's hard. She's officially a failure! And idk what to say about her. I cannot live like this. She's gonna have to do something. She's not strong anymore and she cannot live w/o a man. I'm crying right now and there's so much inside me that I cannot even decide what I'm crying for. I wanna do therapy before I really snap. When I grow up I don't want a man! I wanna be very independent and stand up for women like my mother. I feel like she is giving up on life itself. It's really sad to see my mom like this. I think I miss Deezy? I'm not sure yet but I think I do! I'm really pushing myself but I can only push so far w/o support! I feel like I have no support in most cases and I know I wanna be something and that's the only thing that's motivating me not to give up like my mom. I need God and I am currently forming a relationship with him. I'm so proud. I really don't think people understand what I go through. People don't understand that I literally cry every day! Nobody knows that I talked to a counselor alone because my mom told me I couldn't do it. She doesn't understand that I actually think about giving up on life a lot! And I don't wanna end up like one of those depressed people with fucked up childhoods and I'm not. I know I don't want that life. I want to be the one that prove statistics* *wrong!! I'm gonna try and release some of this steam off by talking to my daddy. He's the last resort, I guess."*

That feeling was confusion. It will be so hard to identify how you feel these days, because there seems to be a buildup of those feelings. However, more than anything, it's confusion. You cannot seem to understand the things that happen around you, but that will not stop you from trying to. It will take time for you to see that the life you were given, was given for a purpose. You will eventually be able to see the why behind the things that affected you. Just keep holding on to whatever faith that you may have.

* * *

04/09/2010: "Life's pretty good right now. I know you're probably tired of these emotional roller-coaster rides. One day I'm happy, the next I'm the saddest person in the world. I don't know what it is, but that's how my life works I guess. I've been really working on my relationship w/ God and I'm trynna get "right" I guess. I'm gonna try out for the cheerleading team and I've been doing pretty good in school. My mom is cool right now, love her to death, but still mad she's not working. My brothers are still my life and everything is everything. I love my school still and my friends and that's about it."

* * *

04/12/2010: "Well well well. Life is still pretty good. The weather is getting nice and schools about to be out! My favorite time of the year. Anyhow, me and ma dukes is doing pretty good, but she still worshiping the ground he walks on. Which really annoys me. I mentioned how close me and God were getting and church was great yesterday. My mom haven't been but I've been the last couple weeks (4 weeks to be exact). Maybe if she see me picking up my act and getting it together she'll wanna do the same. I don't really talk to a lot of people anymore at all. Portage kinda got me isolated. I've become very anti-social which is usually not me! I've opened up to a couple people at Northern and once I try out for the cheer team, everything should get better. I think. I am really lonely again! Anyhow, there are nooooo other boys. I don't even flirt with anyone because I have no one to flirt with! Other than all that I'm pretty good. I've been thinking about my future A LOT! I wanna be a psychologist, but I also wanna turn you into a book. So that's one of my dreams and goals now. I really wanna write a book so everyone can see that w/ all life's problems, you could still make it to the top! I'm going to Chicago in two weeks and I'm gonna talk to my dad and have a serious talk. I think that'd help me a lot. I just noticed that I've been writing to you for a whole year and two months."

Your desire to influence and change people has no healthy balance and it will eventually catch up to you. Speaking about your mother is done so in a manner of "what you have to do" in order for her to change. This is not a healthy space you are in, although it feels like everything is going good. While it is great to want change for the betterment of yourself, you will have to acknowledge that you are not the answer to people outgrowing their toxic and flawed ways.

* * *

04/14/2010: "I don't even know what to say. I don't know if I'm depressed I don't know anything right now. Pain and tears has been my best friend these last couple weeks. Gryphon Place is at my school this week and they've been talking about suicide, depression, and crisis a lot. In fact that's been the main topic. I've thought about suicide multiple times and it's really sad. I push myself and I have no one else to help but I push myself to know that it's wrong and I pray that fate never leads me that way. I really wanna go to counseling because I know I'm not crazy and I'm pushing myself to do better. I'm using positive coping skills and I've never thought about it like that. I just always think about what would the world be like? And I think I'm stressing even more because I don't wanna grow up like this. I wanna be NORMAL! I don't wanna be in no crazy home or going to therapy. I wanna be as happy as I could be. I think it hurts me more to not cuss my mom out than to hurt her feelings. I really wanna tell her about herself but I can't and I just don't understand her. Why is she choosing to live the life she's living? I don't think I'll ever get it. I can't wait 'til I'm old enough to get a job and take care of myself! Today she said a lot of things to me that made me just wanna tell her about heself. She made me realize how bad I was hurting on the inside. One thing that I really wanted to react on was the fact that she called me fake! She said I wanted to be like other people and she being real got us where we are today. Well if being real got us HERE?! Then I wanna be the fakest person in the world. We are not happy, AT ALL. And I need help because this is how I felt when I first got you. This is not the best feeling in the world. Jesus I really don't understand. Every time I think about getting my life together everything gets super worse and nothing goes right. I don't even feel like writing anymore. I just feel down."

You are able to identify at this point that you feel lonely. You do not understand how detrimental mental health is at this age. This is apparent in the way you speak of receiving therapy as well as your mom's "choosing" to live life the way that she was. Therapy does not mean you are "crazy." Seeking it means, that you are sane enough to recognize that something is not right. You will also grow to understand that your mom is battling a mental illness. She is not choosing to give up. The sooner you recognize this, it may save you all's relationship from further damage. It may be a good time for you to use that influencing attitude to suggest that you all receive help as a family. This may or may not work, but at least attempting can help your mom see that you all know and feel everything that is going on around you.

* * *

05/09/2010 (Mother's Day): "So today is like a regular day to me. Nothing sparks me to do anything or feel that this day is special anymore. Like I don't even care. I went to Chicago like two weeks ago and I had fun. I stayed at my dad's but I seen a lot of my family and it was fun. I seen my auntie and I really love her. Okay, so I plan on getting a new notebook soon. We have a really short time together. It's like saying goodbye to my best friend. There's only four more pages of writing in you so I thought about letting my auntie read you this summer. As well as letting her know about my book plan. But I'm not sure because this is like giving my life over to someone. I trust my auntie 100% but I don't know if I'm ready *for her to know about some things. I think I can change people's lives by making you into a book because if I was depressed and I read you, I'd wanna change. Well anyway, I made the J.V. cheer-leading team, which I'm so excited about but I don't know if I'm going to have a lot of support. I've been thinking about that a lot too. That maybe I won't have a lot of support, but I'm gonna do it, and I'm not gonna quit because I can't be a quitter. My mom has been making me wanna do good? Maybe her depressed sad a** life might be needed for me to keep my head up. Maybe that's the reason I'm so determined to do good. I'm gonna set an example for her. I'm gonna cheer, get a job, and just keep myself up and maybe, just maybe she'll wanna get her life together, but then again, it might only make her more jealous and everything else more worse, but it's worth giving it a try. Well there's a secret that I haven't yet shared with you. I've smoked weed three times! Last night was the third! But it's just for fun. Nothing else. I will not end up like my mother. Weed will not be my life. It's just fun, but I do need to stop myself though. Before it gets too far which I doubt because it's not addicting to me at all! Our journey together is almost over and it's kinda sad lol. Well life is good. No boys and it's been like that for a cou-ple weeks. Alex, another person I'd like to introduce. She's my best friend and I love her. I trust her with a lot and she knows a lot about me.*

P.s. I feel like death is nearby. I don't know why I feel that way but I keep feeling like me, or my 3 brothers, or my mom is gonna die. Or like the world is about to end. I really don't wanna feel like this. I hate it. But I know God is by our side and watching over us."

* * *

05/10/2010: "Well today was a pretty good day, other than the fact that I was about to fight three boys...Anyhow I need to release a couple things. First off you can't be a crackhead and a mother at the same time. If she think she finna stiff powder every two weeks and then when she's sober tell me what to do and act like a mom she got sh*t f*cked up. I ain't finna obey, respect, or care for a crackhead! She wonders why she ain't get no love on mother's day! F*ck a mother and a day! She also had the nerves to ask me what's the difference between her and my auntie smoking and drinking, b*tch my auntie ain't on crack! I don't care what she's doing, as long as she supporting me, being there, and ain't smoking crack she'll be better than my mom. Which is honestly sad! I can't wait! 3 more years seems like such a long time. I just wanna be away from her like nobody stress me out more than her."

You still do not understand your feelings, so a lot of it comes out in such hateful ways. The sooner you are able to recognize what it is that you are feeling, the sooner you will be free from this level of hurt. You will grow beyond this mindset. Although it will get rougher before smoothing out, just do not give up. At this time, you aren't going to see things clear enough to understand, but let my words guide you on the path of light. Those internal dark spaces don't extend forever.

* * *

05/12/2010: "Okay, this probably the last entry I have and on to a new journal I go. I always believed from the time I started writing that the last page would be the happiest page with no problems and them all solved. Well, I was sadly wrong! I am just soooo *tired and stressed out. Like I don't even know, I'm f*cking speech-less. I've written all I can write about being sad, like seriously. I'm sick of this low-life, miserable, b*tch of a mother. I'm sick of living this life, I'm sick of not having any support, I'm sick of my dad, I'm just so f*cking sick! I have no support from any direction! Like this is beyond crazy whatever I do and whenever I do it I have no fam-ily support, like no one is here for me! I'm my own motivation, I support my f*cking self in everything I do! I get no support for being in Jeter's Leaders and I just made the cheerleading team and guess who cares? My mom wonders why my friends come first?!? They're the only ones that care and support everything I do no matter what it is. My family is my downfall. Especially my mom. She brings me down more than any hater I know. This b*tch always bringing up how she struggling and I'm no help...B*TCH it ain't my fault that you got fired and you don't wanna do NOTHING with your life. I ain't tell you to live the life you living so I don't give two f*cks about what you're going through. It ain't my f*cking problem. She wants me to not get involved in nothing and live this poor a** low class girl life...NO! I want more for myself and I'm gonna do stuff because I don't wanna end up like her! And I won't! She strug-gle with EVERYTHING that's got to do with her kids but when it comes to going to get weed, sniff crack, drink, go f*ck somebody's man, or to be triflyn with her friends? It's no problem. She do every-thing she gotta do to be a f*cking disgust bucket. When I get older I don't give a f*ck what happens to her. I'm gonna be so rich and she won't get any love from me or anything else. I know God wants us to honor our parents, but she's did nothing to help me be success-ful. And if I make it, it's because I was here for myself with no one by my side. My mom can honestly die and go to hell! Once again,* *this is my last entry until I get a new book, but our journey is something like over. It'll still be like I'm writing to you just a different book. You've helped a lot without you journal, ohhh, where would I be! I'd probably be in a crazy home, but thankfully Mrs. J and my counselor introduced me to you.*

Yours truly, Imani Watson"

This is a result of you being exposed to more than what is appropriate at the time. You are in such a hateful state because you do not understand how to interpret all of the things that you are being exposed to at this time. So you develop feelings and thoughts surrounded by what you believe to be right and wrong. I would advise you to try seeing things from a different light if you have not already. It will also aid you in feeling less frustrated at this age with what was happening around you.

* * *

10/11/2011: "Boy boy boy. It has been a very long time. I haven't wrote to myself in almost, maybe a year. I lost the urge to write once I lost one of my journals. I was thinking about giving writing up and my whole book idea. I wish I could find that whole book because it includes a large chapter of my life. To summarize that book Dairy, my best friend was introduced. Jer and a couple other people were also. One of these days I'll replace it and just write it as an old time I guess. Well life is hard to explain at this moment because you've missed so much. I'm getting, well I've gotten way stronger, emotionally than my normal self. Like wayyyy stronger, but at this specific moment in time I'm not feeling the best way. Today I thought about a lot of things I haven't thought about and

I'm trying to get all these tears out but it's hard because I'm at a happy point in my life. I'm just having a slight downfall and it's not enough to make me cry, it's like I'm too strong but I want to cry, like desperately. I haven't cried in like a month or two which is not normal. I might go back and read my first journal tonight because I need to cry. School is back in and I didn't write during the whole summer, but boy was it a hectic summer. I know when I grow up I'll be fine because I get so much better as the days go on. Anyhow major events have occurred. Like the fact that I'm not friends with Bee or Dannie. And I can't ever see us being friends again. I live with Kay, I think I'm pregnant, but I would rather not go in depth with any of these events. I don't think I need therapy, but I would love to have a daily consultant. I just thought I'd start somewhere and this is a start for me. A start for journaling again.

Imani Watson"

* * *

10/11/2011: "Okay this is ridiculous. I'm not sad but something in me is trying to make me sad. Like my head thinking of all the shit that has personally affected me, but I've forgiven people and situations so I can't be sad but I just feel like I should be! I thought I would also just write down how my mom's boyfriend came on to me and she still deals with him. I just really wish I could have a break down right now because I need it desperately."

You are struggling to feel the emotion because at this point it has been embedded in you that it is better to suppress your emotions. You struggle in this area because you are blocking a natural emotion to occur, which is hurt. You have a right to be hurt and to face your pain. It also becomes an issue, because you won't use your voice. You want someone to help you deal with these tornado of emotions, but you fear sharing your story. Believe it or not, it will be this story that sets you free. At this point in life you are about to be 16 years old. You have moved out of your mom's and in with a cousin. Following this not working out, you end up living with friends back and forth when you and your mom were not doing well. Losing a journal is a result of how unstable your life is at this point. Instead of suppressing the emotion, let it out and acknowledge that things are not ok. While you never went back to write what these times were like in detail, they entailed a lot of fights, boys, smoking, drinking, a suicide attempt, your experience with your mom's boyfriend, and feeling unsupported in all aspects. All of these things that would lead any average 16 year old to be in a space of hurt.

* * *

12/28/2011: "Ok. It's been like 3 months since the last time I wrote and I think that's a huge problem. Right now I'm going through a tough time. I really don't know why I'm so sad, but maybe it's because my birthday is so close. I'm so alone like more alone than I've been since 8th grade. I just feel like all I need is a little encouragement and/or for someone to just say "don't give up." And not because I want them to but because they genuinely don't want to see me give up. I've lost everyone that was close to me. Everyone who I confided in and everyone that I thought would be here until the very end. It started with Ra. She moved to Atlanta and turned into someone I don't know. And it hurts to not have my other half. Me and my mom were starting to build a relationship, *but she's back with him and our relationship is slowly falling apart again. I hate to see everyone exit my life and for no reason at that. I feel like I'm a good person and I make a lot of sacrifices physically and emotionally to satisfy everyone. It's just hard for me to understand I guess and I just hate the feeling I have. Me and Dannie's friendship will never be the same. I highly appreciate everything she does and has done, but with my trust being so f*cked up adding to what she did to me, we'll never be able to be as close as we were. She is /was someone, in fact the only someone that I can trust with my life. Like I even let her read my journals and for her to f*ck me over for a guy was just beyond foul. Then there's Dairy and I know I've already written about this but I can't get over it because I thought out of everyone he'd never leave my side. He made up for all the time my older brother missed and it just helped to have that male figure so close, but like everyone else he hit the exit. Maybe it's because I'm too sad. Idk, because I just can't figure out why no one can just be here for me. Kay is next. She took me in and all that and I appreciate it and even started trusting her, but just like the rest she broke it. Like, sometimes I wonder, is it me? Like is there something I did/do because I just don't f*cking get it. And me being the person I am I've let someone new in my life. We've been friends for a month now and she's really cool. We actually had an instant click and she's helped me out so much in the last month. I like to believe she's the one person who is still loyal and there aren't any signs that she isn't, but I still have my guards up just because I've been amazed by people a little too much. I'm gonna end it right there with people exiting my life though because that alone can turn into a whole book. Beyond that, taking care of myself is becoming hard and complicated as hell. I've came along way in three years feeling* *alone. I do feel like it is way too late to give up, but I've never felt like this, all the time that I've been alone. And I have the option of moving to Chicago, but as I've written before I would lose a lot. And my biggest fear is losing the Kalamazoo Promise Scholarship that I have in place. I don't want to put my education at risk but when I say "hard," I mean this sh*t is no joke. And I'm not looking for sympathy because that's not what I need, but I do need/want help because I think it's f*cked up that I've had to teach myself half the sh*t I have on my own. I don't want to get help though because I feel like people will get the wrong impression and think its sympathy that I'm looking for. And don't confuse me, when I say it's hard. I don't only mean financial wise. I mean on every level it is hard. Being 16 and doing literally everything on your own is not the easiest thing to do. I am strong though. That I can give myself, because I can't count how many times I've stopped my own self from ending it and okay I had like a downfall and attempted the dumb shit I did last year, but I'm still here and I really think that's the only thing that really matters. I know I always saying I'm going to get back on my normal writing schedule, but I really am because I hate having to cram things in like this. I feel like when I wait forever to write I leave out a lot and my entries don't really make sense. That's my new year's resolution. I'm going to get back on my regular schedule for writing because it helps a lot. Like right now I feel 10x better than I did 2 hours ago. I know I do a lot of crying and stressing, but I like to think that just maybe it'll all pay off and one day I'll be happy My thoughts are all over the world right now and it shouldn't be hard to tell with this entry, but I'm going to get caught up on my writing, because there's so much missing.*

xoxox, Imani Watson"

So much time passes by and everything will eventually start feeling like a blur. At this time you may be feeling like you are an empty soul occupying a body. To know that you are surrounded by people and feel like you are the loneliest person on earth is not abnormal. What you are feeling now is not atypical. But as you stated yourself, it is far too late to give up at this point. Have faith in something strong enough that you will continue to thrive beyond all that life puts in front of you. You are a good person, you are not "too sad," and it is not you. There's a lot going on at this time with you. So much that you will find it hard to put into words. Just breathe. Using writing as a coping skill will work for you, but you will have to learn how to stop letting life distract you from this therapeutic craft.

* * *

09/10/2012: "The last time I wrote a journal was October of last year. My. My. My where the hell has time went? I re-read through a couple logs and have come to the conclusion that I don't even want to publish a book. I would just love a book (unpublished) to share with everyone I've ever encountered in life. Now the reason that it took me so long to get in the spirit is because I have been and seen almost everything during my time of not writing. Two days ago, my auntie poochie (Sharon) died. It hit me a tad bit hard being the fact that I found out about the cancer the day she found out she had lumps in her breast. Kills my soul that I just talked to her during the summer and she stressed how much she loved me. She even gave me money for being beautiful. My family is holding up well, but everyone's hurting, everyone. We're not used to losing *people to death, especially not a close aunt like my auntie poochie. I hope her precious soul is resting like it's never rested before. I sat in a bathroom stall at work yesterday evening and realized that I partially lost myself. Why is it that I've went a year without writing and it's what was my first love? Exactly. Welp, anyways, D is GONE. My mom finally woke up out of the daze she was in! She is a working woman and doing the best she's been doing since we've moved to Kalamazoo. I love my mom. I don't understand how we ever went through the bullsh*t she's ever put us through. She is a strong woman and it still hurts to say she let herself go for 5 years because that 5 years damaged me in ways I can't even begin to explain. Don't get me wrong, they also put the ambition I have in my veins. I'm not the average 17 year old girl at all. I don't think like the normal human. I swear I don't and who's to say that's wrong. I don't know, but because of our f*cked up world it is deemed "abnormal." Which is why I believe I'm damaged, just partially. I didn't have the normal 13-17 year old life and I still don't think I'll ever have a normal life because of the fact that my strong lady let herself go for men. I hope D and Man find their selves and I give my best wishes to them. I've found that to find happiness, you have to let go of resentment and give forgiveness. They f*cked my family up, but I'm letting it go. Right here, right now. LMAO, so I was gonna start my next section on friends, but F*CK A FRIEND! I don't know if Tish was ever mentioned in any journals but I met a Tish. We became closer than me and Bee in 08-09 days. Well at least that's what I had liked to think. Let's see why are me and the majority of my friends not friends anymore? Because they decided having a d*ck would be better than our friendship. Right? You know I would never do half the sh*t people do to me, to them. I* *just don't have it in me. F*ck time, Tish was my f*cking sister and I loved and still do love her dearly, but she just contributed to f*cking my trust up as everyone else I've ever put my faith into and thought they'd be there for me. You know, I still don't know if she's forgiven because she acts so blind to the fact that I know everything that's ever went on behind my back. I know, pretty contradictive, but hey, I didn't say I was 100% in self happiness. At the same time I resent that girl for helping f*ck up my mind and train of thought. Thank her, at the same time. I believe fate brought her in my life to link me and my best friend/sister/mentor Kee. Just when you think your life was hell, I promise there is someone who had it just like you if not worse. Kee has been in my life for no longer than a year and for the first time in 17 years I feel like the loyalty I'm giving out is being returned. It's been so long since I wrote so I don't know who I've added but the people I f*ck with and got it if I got it would be Kee, family, Reb, Morg, Kan, Von, D, Tay, Bee, Mesha, Des, Ashlee, Don, and that's about it. Of course there are a host of other people that show me love and I show them love, but the people previously mentioned, can't even be put into words how much I love them. I wonder if all this emotion has been put into me because my time is coming or it needed to come out on paper, or in some form or way. For the last few days I've been enhanced with the highest level of emotion a person could ever receive. They say if you love someone, let it go, and if it comes back it means so much more, right? I know I've wrote this about other guys who I swore I was in love with and blahhhh blahhh blahh..I left J alone for this one. Desmond. I don't think he knows or ever will know the amount of myself I would give for/to him. I don't even want to begin to explain our story because I think it's too deep to go into for my first entry about him. Any-*

ways, as predicted, he's not here and made me fall just so he could not be here. That's the next chapter though. Desmond along with Tish can get their own chapters and so do J, being that they were the last three people that hurt me so f*cking much and got me dropping tears. Anyone that has read my journals will know that Kalamazoo has ruined my life in more than one way. I applied to Spelman College, in the middle of applying to Clark Atlanta, and also North Carolina A&T. I'm out of this b*tch the day I get the chance. F*CK KALAMAZOO. I can't wait to attend college to prove all these b*tches wrong and beat f*ck a** statistics! Man I just wanna feed everybody I love!! I have to make it, like I am obligated to do so. When I turn 18 I will begin working on my book...I wanna call it "The Longest Road" or something in that nature. I forgot to add to the list of names, I love Ti for being the wonderful friend person she is. If anything were to just happen to me, I'd want her to know I feel like I owe her and I love her! Hope she never changes and keeps talking. Welp I just had to make a brief comeback. I will not take another break, seriously. Too much has went unwritten.

Xoxoxo, Imani Watson"

This is another example of how your mind is constantly all over the place and how you lacked stability. Because you do not have a designated source of emotional support, you are trying to figure everything out and how to cope with things that are going on in your world, alone. The sooner you breathe, the sooner your life will become manageable. This entry contains a lot of "dropping off." You are finding things to drop the responsibility of your emotions off on. For example, your mothers choice of men, your friendships, a boy, and even the city that you live in.

Find ways to release this. Release the thought of having a situation to make responsible for your emotions. Be that source of control that you are looking for in all other things. Being able to attest from a different point of view, I believe that the sooner you take control of your emotions, the sooner you will have a breakthrough. Life will continue to be your best teacher, so learning how to accept and release will become your saving grace. This is an important moment, because this is the last time as a "child" that you are putting pen to paper in order to sort through your life experiences. Carrying all of this through your adulthood and covering it with a blanket will not leave you in a good space. Address these things early on or you will eventually be forced to deal with them when you are least prepared."

Chapter 4: I think I'm ok

02/14/2013: "I'm a tad bit tired. So I can't write much tonight but I did my first blog entry today and I am extremely proud of myself. The level of support was beyond me. I truly didn't expect it. I just hope the fake love doesn't start here. All bullsh*t aside I thought I would stop writing when I turned 18 and just started working on a book but that's no longer what I want to do. I'm going to write until I graduate then it'll be more meaningful that way because at the end of the road I actually accomplished something, you know? So yeah, I missed a few months, well more than a few of writing but I look at it like this, if I didn't write about it, there's no significance because more than likely trying to write about something that happened 3-4 months ago won't have much emotion to it. So I'll start from here until May. I'm sure it'll be interesting enough and if I have to fill in then I will. I'm going to try and stay consistent due to the fact that I actually started my blog."

* * *

02/16/2013: "*I'm drunk. This is a first time...being drunk and writing. I wonder if my thoughts will be even more truthful because they say a drunk man, speaks sober thoughts. I wonder who came up with that sh*t and how does he know. Anyways, I have a ton of sh*t on my mind right now. My mind is literally all over the place. I've been working on the blog and people love it, but I figured out today if I plan on making a book, I can't spill everything. So I'm unsure of how to submit the post. I need to talk to my English teachers. Anyhow, I'm good, like I feel myself growing into a wonderful person, seriously. I'm figuring out what matters and what doesn't, at least I think I am. Right now, what I can't seem to stop thinking about is Desmond and Meg. I lost two very important people and I really do not know how to handle the sh*t. In real life, me and Meg did EVERYTHING together. Like I didn't breathe w/o her. I told her things that I was afraid to admit to myself about life and sh*t. She dipped for a relationship. Lost the realest friendship I thought I had known, for a relationship. It just f*cks me all up. I haven't talked about it to anyone and don't really plan on it. I just can't believe someone I gave 100% loyalty to betrayed me. Makes me question everything. Then aside from her, I lost Desmond. I don't know if he is my soul mate, but I sure don't picture a better feeling or a deeper love. He has a girlfriend now and I'm salty. I think he's really done with me. I did some f*cked up sh*t. After tonight I don't think I want to drink anymore. Even though I feel like I've let go of grudges, I still feel a feeling of anger in my heart and it's like everything triggers me. Sometimes I wonder if I'll ever relapse and want to die again because according to statistics, it's possible. Even though I'm excellent right now.*"

* * *

02/20/2013: "*It's amazing to see how much I've changed and how different my mindset is from 3-4 years ago. If I knew back then, what I know now, as cliché as it sounds, I would've definitely done things a lot differently and I would've probably had different thoughts. It makes me mad that I lost a whole journal because it's a whole year missing and I'm mad that I didn't stay consistent when things got rough because that's almost another year and all I have are the memories in my head. Which isn't a bad thing, but I'm sure I felt different about these things during the actual time. I went back and read all of my journal entries yesterday and I realized something in doing so. I was indeed a lost child and I contradicted myself, and I wrote so many things out of anger. Said so many things, wished so many things, that I wouldn't even think of these days. Stuff was so mind blowing that I even almost considered not to blog anymore because it's almost like I'm scared for people to see how angry I used to be. Lately I been all over the place with my mind. Not necessarily in a bad way, but I've had a sh*t ton on my brain. When reading my journals, I noticed that I talked sh*t about people I have forgiven and that have proved they aren't what I thought they were. And I can't figure out if I should put them out in the blog. It's like is it fair to them to know that I thought such harsh things? Or is it fair to me to keep it bottled up and never let them understand the damage they've caused? It's so confusing, and then my mother, we have such a good relationship and it f*cks me up that once in my life I had the level of hate for her that I did. Not necessarily taking the blame it's just like I don't get how life let her do what she did to me and my life. Even though it's all in the* *past, it still feels weird that I was hurt by so many people I loved and still love today. My dad? Now? He's like my best friend and being young and not understanding that everything he did was for my sake almost makes me hate myself for saying some of the things I have ever said to or about him. Going back and reading all of the things I said about my parents just...idek it just helps me realize how much things have changed and how much emotionally stronger I am as an individual. Also going back and reading my journals I realized how much I had forgot. It brought back a lot of emotions and there was a ton of stuff I forgot about. How is beyond me. I got so scared I didn't even want to write this. Idk how to explain it. I just wish my childhood could have been different. If I wasn't so lost and confused and angry at the time, I don't think I would have chosen some of the things I did and not to say I'm not extremely thankful for where I made it to, but why did it take for me to experience the worst sh*t. Reading all of my old journals brought a lot of unanswered questions back. That's all, just questions. I took my anger out on so many of the wrong people and it's crazy to think about. It makes me wanna go back and be stronger. I mean having the mindset that I have now with not letting much phase me and me worrying only about me."*

This comes off so powerful because the emotion is so easy to feel. It is another one of the roller coasters where you go from one extreme to the next. Still being lost and feeling like you are figuring things out will have you in a space of fighting yourself on who and what to put first. You are making progress in your journey and learning, as this is a clear moment of you going behind your black curtain. You point out some of your own weaknesses, but leave out one that you have instead painted clearly in this entry. You have been taught to put others before yourself, so this idea of putting yourself last feels like the right thing to do because anything else comes off as selfish. Being so far removed from the idea of putting yourself first, you will find yourself in situations where you are doing more self-harm and destruction. The sooner you learn the put yourself first, the more freedom you will experience. It will be a hard cycle to break, but it will be broken. Putting yourself first is just as important as any other life value. Society, especially the one that you are attached to has taught you that you do not come first. Do not allow the task of undoing a thought process, stop you from your growth. I also want you to take this time to acknowledge your growth and be proud that even when you were still in the storm, you found ways to address and overcome bad habits of your own.

* * *

10/02/2013: "It's getting closer to my time to start putting this thing into a final draft. Ahhhh. Just a thought. Anyhow, man oh man has sh*t been real or has it been real??? I absolutely cannot deal. Well, where shall I start? Myself. I am so happy that it's literally driving me crazy. My heart is full of joy, but my mind is like, "no, this isn't right, be mad." I just can't find it in me. In fact, I'm so happy I could cry because I didn't expect to be this happy and the other tears would come from shock. Going deeper in, why am I shocked by people's actions or people being able to just get up and walk out of this life of mine? Why on earth am I shocked? No one can answer that. It's almost like they were put there to help me realize what life is truly about and to help me find myself, figure out *who I really am. I haven't known myself in years...I am literally drowning in my tears, how could I have been so blind to myself? That makes me feel a way that's a tad bit hard to explain. My only question would be, if they were put there to help me figure out who I am, why on earth did I have to make so many good memories with them. I thank Tish and Desmond with everything my body has in it. Even though their intentions weren't at all to help out, they did exactly that. I'm just a little upset that it happened how it did. Kinda f*cked up that the two people I last put my whole trust in, ended up to be like the rest of the world. For a solid second I thought she was my friend, my sister, a part of me, and then just like that she's against me. I thank the b*tch for being disloyal and taking his side. Had to realize misery literally loves company and birds of a feather, flock together. They need each other. I don't need either one of them and I'm just so thankful I got to meet them and have them teach me more about who I am. In a way Tish helped me enhance my loyalty skills. Even though she doesn't know it. I don't wish her bad luck and I don't wish her good. I could care less if we ever said two words to each other again. Don't get me wrong, in the midst of her teaching me who I am, the b*tch had me low and lost trynna figure out why or how, but f*ck her. Desmond, ehhh...If I want anything in life I want him to see how happy I am without him. He taught me the biggest lesson ever learned. Learned a lot about myself dealing with him. MAN! It couldn't have been love or you know maybe it was, but he was more of a downfall than a progress. I let him do me any kind of way without even realizing I was being treated wrong. I don't regret any minute we spent together though. Helped both of us out. Taught him that he liked girls that made him respect them. I learned that I need to make sure I'm* *always getting the respect I deserve to get. I let that boy disrespect me in more ways than one. F*cked up, but I'm only 17 right? I'm in my learning stage. I don't have it all. Other than seeing me happy, I want Desmond to know how much he's taught me. I'm gonna tell him before I leave for school next summer. I'll make sure he knows! Then he made a statement like we had sex too fast. I can't explain what that did to me. One, it helped me understand that the world is not always how you see it. I didn't see it like that. I thought it was just that we clicked off back but that obviously wasn't the case. Made me feel real low. So now that I've decided I don't wanna have sex again. I've never wanted to be considered "easy" or a "hoe," cause I promise that's not me, but that got me though. His buddy made it seem like basically he called me a hoe, so I attempted to embarrass him and I believe it worked. As bad as it sounds, that's what got me to thinking that they were meant to be a lesson. They're not worth any more of my energy or tears. Whatever happens in life though, I'll never forget the last few months of my life. I literally lost everyone in the blink of an eye and changed my number. It's just a battle of emotions in me. I'm still regrouping myself from it all like I can't believe I was lost these last few years. Accepting anything, settling for anything, letting people walk over me, looking for all the wrong things, and not valuing myself. It just f*cks me up that they had to be the ones to help me see that because I know they didn't have any good intentions and still don't. I can almost guarantee they don't see it how I do though. Gahhhhh...besides that I'm really content. I know I've said it before, but I feel so different and I can honestly say I've been working on me. I mean now that I actually know who I am and who I want to become. A few detours and mistakes but I'm Imani. Who I was last two-three years?*

I don't know. I've never really cared what others thought but I'm really becoming more careless and trying to focus on what satisfies me and my feelings. I find this ironic though, the guy who I put the most emotional energy into, thinks I'm easy, that kind of f*cks me up. I can't wait to tell him how it made me feel and stuff next June. If I don't do anything before I move, I'll be sure to let him know that. I actually hope him and the new girl work out, also because I know I'll eventually find someone later in life and I've always been like that. If I'm happy, I want my exes, old friends, or new ones to be as well. I don't know why I feel so good man. To just know who I am and actually work on that person makes me feel some type of wonderful way.

P.S. I just realized I'm missing a whole notebook! That's a whole chapter of my life forgotten. Maybe once I get going I'll remember it or something."

It is so interesting to see that at this point you thought you had it figured out and that you have found yourself. This is a turning point, in fact a major one, but as time goes on you will learn that you do not know who you are just yet. Life has a funny way of showing us that we are not who we always believe that we are. You'll change and experience so many different things that getting attached to a version of yourself is something to avoid. You will also learn as time goes on that you in fact, do care what people say and think about your actions. You will learn that you have actually spent most of your life being a people pleaser. The sooner you realize that you do not have it all figured out and probably never will, the easier it will be for you walking into your purpose. You will eventually understand why it is ok to not have it all figured out. You will also come to understand why you should not give so much power to situations, such as guys saying "you're easy." Without addressing these things in their entirety, it will lead you back to a similar space later in your life.

* * *

12/20/2014: "Thoughts and feelings. Boy has it been too long. Writing for me does what nothing else in this world could do. I mean nothing else can stop the urge to run out in the middle of the road and invite the biggest truck to RUN ME OVER. I'm better. Much better than before, but that doesn't stop these days where I feel like I have absolutely no control over my life. When I stop writing, I always make plans to start back again, I always say "I'm gonna write down what happened today," but I obviously never do, for at least a year. I wish I wrote more, I think I'd be an even happier person. I am happy, happier than before but I think I'd be much happier. Welp, right now I'm sitting at work, frustrated to the maximum, trying to figure out what I want to do. I think I wanna break up with my boyfriend who I have dedicated 3 years of my life to, but I also think it'd be a not so smart move. I think I want a second job, but I know it'll be overwhelming. I think I wanna lay in bed for the next 11 days and not even bother to celebrate my birthday, but I know I'll end up in depression. I think I want to unmeet everyone I have met in the last five years, but I've met a few great people. I think I wanna do a lot of things and it's driving me crazy. I wish, I think I want to do things, but I never know what's best so I just stop thinking about what I wanna do and do whatever happens if that makes sense. I feel so silly writing right now because it's been so long. I also feel bad, because I feel silly.

Writing is probably the only reason I'm still alive and well. I don't see why I only feel comfortable writing when I'm hurting. Its... I don't even know. Just weird.

Ps: my coworker is making me want to smack the f*ck out of her. I wish she goes away, like really."

* * *

04/26/2015: "Sometimes I just sit & I stare & I reminisce on all the crazy sh*t I've been through. It's scary. Scariest thing in the world to still be standing, to still be prospering as an individual, & to still be able to smile. Nothing in the world scares me more. Sometimes I feel invincible. Like why can't I break, why am I so strong, how do I get through these things. I'm 20 years old. Just 20, & I have seen just about EVERY thing life has to offer besides death. If I could've lived the years 4-7 for the rest of my life I would be beyond content. So innocent, clueless, & careless. Genuine smiles, genuine happiness, filling me up so effortlessly. & then at six, you realize when the "baby sitter" is taking advantage of you that your mom is addicted to the streets. That she would rather get drunk & party, rather than keep you home, under her wing, where no one can harm you. & then every weekend being scared for your life while your aunt & uncle are drunk off their a**es, fighting, yelling, & leaving you unattended to sneak off & do lord knows what. There were never any words said between me & my brother but I know he felt my hurt, my fear, my confusion. He was always too busy jumping off things to realize that our situation wasn't right. Turning 8 & being able to say I've seen my grandma smoke out of a crack pipe. Then being disciplined whenever I walked in on it. F*cking crazy right? Well not the craziest thing. Me & my brother *sitting on the porch after my mom decided not to give my aunt food stamps. We were sat on the porch with our bags to wait for my mom, who had no intention on showing up. May I remind you that it's night time & we're in the safest place on earth...the south side of Chicago. A black car pulls up & men dressed in all black jump out, take the kid who is standing on the corner, beats him & throws him in the trunk. Or an even better one, how about the time when my mom picked up a stalker. That was fun. Staying at different people's house every night, because it was just too unsafe to go home. & when we did go home, his truck always waiting in the front. It's funny to look at now but as an 8 year old girl, imagine the flush of fear I had everyday wondering if this man would kill us. & you haven't even heard the most f*cked up part. My mom finally decided that she's had enough & we are leaving Chicago. By having enough, she's pregnant with the third kid by the third man & we have to get as far away from him as possible. We spend a year in Minnesota, not much there. I became a Buddhist, my mom flipped, & I never prayed to Buddha again. Funny to think about now. I was a Buddhist at 10. Minnesota wasn't all that great & we decided to come to Michigan. Absolute WORST decision my mom has ever made in her life. This is when the sh*t starts. To begin the f*cked-upness. My mom starts dating our cousin. Shortly after, he moves in with us. & shortly after that they're snorting powder together. & shortly after that he's beating the living daylight out of her on a weekly basis. The hate I acquired for him was unspeakable. Every night I wanted to kill him. I plotted, I planned, & I practiced. I can't blame him for the reason my mother decided to put him before us, do drugs, & neglect us. However, back then he was nothing less than the blame. In my eyes he* *ruined life as I knew it. I still in some ways feel that way. Except now I think my mom played a bigger role. That's who owed her all to me. Not him. Anyways, he came in, I remember her trying to explain to me the f*cked up situation about how she was screwing her cousin. It was the sickest thing I had ever heard of, the first time I was embarrassed to be her child. The first two years in Michigan were bad, but it got worst. We moved. House to house for the first 4 years. Every house creating more & more f*cked up memories. I eventually invited depression in at age 13. It was the night my mom came tumbling down the stairs into my bedroom followed by this monster kicking her. I ran to get the phone, he unplugged them. I tell my friend from school not to panic. Ha! Not to panic when she'd just met me & she was witnessing my mom get beat down by this man. Somehow we escaped outside, my mom running down the street half naked screaming "help!" It was in that very moment, that the world was at a pause. I put the night so far in the back of my head that I often forget the unbearable feeling. The feeling that you get when you think no pain in the world can POSSIBLY be greater than this. I just remember the tears. There were so many tears. I'm staring at my mom, but I don't see her, I hear her screaming for help, but I don't hear her. I'm standing there dazed, amused, & numb. I knew at this point, life would never be the same. Living in Kalamazoo ruined me. Broke me down until I couldn't be broken anymore. When my dad would send for me to go to Chicago for the weekends, I would put every f*cked up thing somewhere deeply hidden in my brain. At 14 I'm battling my mom, physically and literally. She's taking all of her anger out on me, only me. I started journaling. I have journals recalling my f*cked up teenage years. I saw my mom prepare to snort powder.*

I saw my mom give up on us. I saw my mom give up on herself. I saw my mom's soul leave her body. I saw the mom that I once knew, make her exit & she still hasn't come back. I never thought I would be living the life where I come home from school & the lights are shut off or I wake up one morning & the water isn't flowing. When we hit that point, I knew it was completely over for the life we knew. My brothers were always too young to understand. I knew way more than I wanted or needed to know. I knew everything that was happening under our roof & if I dared told anyone I would get beat like I was a random person on the street. At 15, my mom's 3rd boyfriend picked me up from school sloppy drunk & gets us hit by a semi-truck. Knocked off the road, flipped over, and the next thing I remember is my mom coming to get me from the hospital room. At this point I had so much hate for her, I couldn't believe I was still alive. I was mad. This meant that I would still have to pretend that I was happy, still have to take care of three kids, & still have to endure the pain that had built itself inside of me over the years. At 16, my mom's 4th boyfriend in the 5th year that we lived in Michigan came in the bathroom after me. Pushing me against the sink, rubbing his fingers through my hair, with that stupid creepy smile. Saying things like I look good with my hair down, or how good my hair smelt, and how he could buy me whatever. Idk what it was. Maybe the look in my eyes, the sweat, or the thought of my mom walking in, but he just stopped. Just stopped & I closed the door behind him. I locked the door. I undressed myself, I started the shower, & I sat in the tub. I cried so hard that I threw up. I think the tears came from the fact that I knew, when I picked up that phone to call my mom, deep down inside, I knew she would choose him. How did I know? Cause he came on to my cousin

& when she told my mom, my mom accused her of being a liar. Knowing this, I still voluntarily tore my heart to pieces. I called my mom, told her what happened, & her response was "let me call this m*thafucka." I hung up the phone, packed all my clothes & I left. It was the third time I had run away & this time I promised myself I would never go back. I was 16. My mom's boyfriend tried me, I wanted her to kill him, I wanted her to say I'm on my way home, I wanted her to do more than call the m*thafucka. I wanted her to do what she had done in the past. Protect me, make me feel like no one can touch me, be there for me. I wanted her to be a mother. But I definitely wanted too much out of her at the time. As I bounced around house to house for a while. I cried what felt like every night, for a year straight. Mostly silent cries. The ones where you lay in bed, or in my case on the floor, & let tears run down the side of your face, & it feels like something is inside your stomach twisting every organ. The cry where you just stare off at the ceiling & wish you could die. Every day I wanted to call my family in Chicago, call my dad, or call my aunt to come & get me. Everyday. But whenever I thought to, I would think of who my mom was. I would be discouraged thinking no one would help me because she was who she was. I always thought, who would go against her. Who would help me & risk the world of drama she would've brought to their lives so I just stuck it out. I also knew that if I left Michigan I would have no chance at going to college. Deep down inside, there was something in me that wanted to go against the grain, wanted to overcome all the f*cked up sh*t. I eventually started working to care for myself. Some days I walked miles, took rides from random people, friends, cabs. You name it! I let my grades slip one year. The year I decided I no longer wanted to be on this earth, the year I actually felt lost. I

was so good at hiding my pain, that when I got alone it hit so hard. One of my teachers got me talking with a counselor and journaling. That helped more than I would've ever imagined. My teachers were key to me not harming myself. They pen paled with me, they took me out, they talked to me about boys, they checked on me throughout summers. If my mom ever got wind that I was "sad," "hurt," "ruined," "depressed," or anything of the nature she would beat me. She would find me. & she would beat me. Like the game changer at 8am. She found me at one of my friend's house & beat the dog sh*t out of me. She kicked me so hard that I went through the wall. Not metaphorically speaking. I literally put a hole in the wall with my back. She kicked me down a flight of stairs & when she got to me, she beat me like we had never met each other. One of those beatings that blind you & leaves you sitting in whatever spot you're left in until someone approaches you. When I cry now. I cry for my old self. Just sitting here thinking about that day. I wouldn't wish the pain on my worst enemy. Not the pain from the beating, but the emotional pain. I was so damaged on the inside. If I could've walked in the middle of traffic & be killed, I would have. Luckily, I was so stunned that I couldn't leave the house. I was scared, battered, & wanted a hug. I wanted someone to hug me. I wanted to die but at the very same time, I wanted someone to hug me & say everything will be ok. I was tired of calling my aunt. Tired of her listening to me cry over the phone. Tired of running to my best friend. Tired of him picking me up, driving me to a random spot & letting me cry everything in my body out. Tired of him telling me I need to get help. Tired of my teachers playing the role of support. Tired of them feeling sorry for me. Tired of planning to die. Just tired. Because with my aunt, best friend, teachers, program *managers, & anyone else who wanted to understand, could not do anything to save me from my life or mom in all reality. Seeking their sympathy & help in my eyes became so pointless. I gradually got my grades back together. Worked more hours. & started doing normal teenage things. Drinking, smoking, going out, being happy. Even if it meant pretending. Now, in a present world. I'm a junior at a top universities, I've never slept around, I've had the same boyfriend for 3 years. I've lived on my own for 4 years, 2 of those years in my own home. I work full time. I don't believe in excuses. I don't have children. I bought my first two cars by myself. I hate handouts & sympathy. My core depression comes from getting B's rather than As. & when I smile, I feel it. I feel happiness, in my body. My primary focus is finding my truest self. Now wouldn't that scare you? I'm not perfect. I still think about it & cry, I still fuck up, I still make stupid mistakes, etc. But, I live a pretty normal life. Try to imagine all of the things I left out. I skipped years of bullsh*t & still provided a very fucked up story line. I left out the part when my father went to prison my senior year in high school. & the many times I called the police to get my mom off of me. & the time I pulled a knife on my mom's boyfriend & when he removed his hands from her neck, she wanted to fight me. & the time my mom went to jail for months & left me to take care of my brothers. & the time where I stopped eating. & the times I bullied people to relieve myself of pain. For me to only have minor anxiety & feel sad very rarely, is scary. I wrote this note because, I'm scared today. I'm scared that one day I'll wake up & everything that I've been through will be on top of me. Weighing me down & that I'll never get up again. How do I know my past will never come back?"*

* * *

05/16/2015: "Today I woke up and decided that I wanted to take control of my happiness. I find myself waking up, laying in bed, and thinking so negatively these days. I do not know who I am. I do not know who I really am. I mean I know I am Imani, I know I am 20 years old, and I know I work and go to school. I know what I like SOMETIMES and I know what I don't like SOMETIMES. I do not know if this is normal, but I do not like it if it is. I want more, I want better, I want more joy. My goal for the next three months is me. I am making myself my project and dedicating my all to it. I am willing to lose myself, lose people, lose things, and this lifestyle if it means finding my true self and happiness. That is truly the only thing I want out of life right now. It's scary to think about, but I don't wanna turn back or change my mind. When you're tired, you're just tired. I wanna smile and I wanna feel it EVERY TIME. I have some happy days, but I still don't feel the happiness I want. All too often, I'm competing with me, myself, and I. So here's to finding a new me!"

On this journey you will find great versions of yourself, but do not get too attached. Getting attached will get in the way of you continuing to seek higher levels of happiness and greatness within yourself. It is going to seem like one of the hardest tasks, but you do not want to find yourself back in this same exact spot five years later. Make this a continuing journey of working on genuine happiness and peace for yourself no matter how hard it may seem during the present moment.

* * *

05/07/15: "Today I woke up tired for one. As time went on, I felt myself starting to get irritated. One of my biggest pet peeves with myself, is that I am always comparing and contrasting myself with other people. I saw a quote the other day that really touched me in a way, that I cannot wait to feel it 100%. It read, "I have never met a woman that I would rather be." I do not necessarily want to be anyone else, but I want to stop always comparing what I have and what I look like to other people. It drives me crazy.. I do not know the first steps in building my confidence so high that I literally would not want the skin, weave, body, etc. of anyone else in the world. I know it's easier for women in this day and age to want something another woman has like a banging body, a more better looking boyfriend, weave, car, house, etc. but it is not for me. I do not know why I continue to do it, when it makes me so mad that I do. So I know one of my major goals is achieving a higher level of confidence! I cannot wait to see how that pans out for me. Now, I just have to figure out where to start. Cheating is bad. I think. I want to get to a place where I see no wrong or right because I am not the judge of life. BUT, cheating cannot be a good thing? Can it. Well, I think that could be part of the reason I find myself so frustrated these days. What if messing around with J is creating a false sense of happiness for me? What if I don't love him how I believe I do? Then again, what if it's genuine happiness? And what if I really do love him? How do I find these things out for sure? grrr. Last night I decided, that I want to go back to when I did not think of other men and I did not want to cheat. I wonder if I try it for 30 days what will happen....If I go 30 days doing what I had been do-

ing before (being faithful), where will that take me. Will it make me realize I am not happy in my relationship or will it make me realize that I am just being dumb right now? I don't know how to come second, and that is where J places me so that is why I decided to call it off. I am sacrificing a man who wants to do nothing more than make me happy, for a man who occasionally wants to make me happy when he's not with his girlfriend. I do not know about this situation. I did try to leave my boyfriend so I can live a life outside of him, just to see what it is like, but I was forced to experiment that life while still being with him. The thoughts (I will discuss at a later date) that I have been having these past couple days, really makes me want to be single because I feel so dirty, but the only way I will get out of this relationship is if, I walk away and don't look back, but I don't even think I could do that. *sighs* I know this was all scattered, but I get what I'm saying."

Breathe and trust that you will find ways to get over this phase of your life.

* * *

05/09/15: "Yesterday I skipped a day, but I had a fantastic day. I spent it with Desmond and actually did not think of a million other things I would have rather had been doing. We had a really good time and it felt like the old days. We also had a man pay for our food so that contributed to my great day! We also had really good sex last night. So good that I did not even think about J the entire time. I feel myself falling for my boyfriend again and I am super happy about it. I love him. I really do. But for a moment there, he just was not doing the job for me. And it drove me crazy because

I wouldn't really want anyone else to do the job, but at the end of the day, a person can only take so much of nothing but flaws. Anyways, today I woke up in an ok mood, as the day went on I was in a better mood and by night fall my mood seemed to go downward. Thanks to my brain, that does nothing but think. I don't know what my problem is today. Most of my frustration comes from me wanting to see overnight changes within myself. I know it's not how life works but somehow I cannot convince my brain of this. I don't know. But I did notice more things that I would like to change... & as I am writing this it hits me! I should stop focusing on what I want to change about myself. Like, maybe that should not be my PRIMARY focus? hmmm. welp anyways, I'll still make note of what I would like to do better. I think I need to start being 100% honest to myself. I tend to sugarcoat only when it comes to myself. It's almost like I'm scared to hurt myself. I would definitely like to see a change in that because I think it'll help my journey. My mood was a little annoying today, but I'm good. Deep down I feel good to know that I am putting myself first and trying at least..."

* * *

05/11/2015: "Today I woke up, mood matching this gloomy weather. It's like I don't feel good, but I don't necessarily feel bad either. I have a lot on my mind. Today I realized that when one thing goes bad, I think of a million other things to help bring my mood low. I wonder what are steps I can take to not let one thing affect me so drastically. It could be the smallest to the biggest thing. I do not like the feeling. This morning I woke up to an email from my old job telling me that I would not be eligible for re-hire because I was fired. I was never fired. I put my two weeks in an actually had a letter to prove it. It just makes me upset and I cannot even figure out why. After writing it, I actually cannot figure out why I am actually mad. I think it is because I just do not like bad news maybe? Well now that I know I don't have an actual reason to be upset, I suppose I should try to make it go away in my mind and find something more healthy to think about. I had a really relaxing day yesterday. Shonnie and her girlfriend came to visit for us to take them to a concert. Good company & nothing but good vibes. We smoked and laughed and talked and ate good. I was glad to have them. Me and my boyfriend are doing well. I hope we can keep it up. I love it when I feel in love. I woke up today wanting a baby. Something I go back and forth on every single day. Something else I woke up annoyed about is the future. It almost seems that I am so obsessed with how my future will play out. I know I want nothing more than success, but I worry I am not taking the proper steps. This is a time where I wish I can take everything day by day. Like, I am allowing something that isn't even near stress me out. That comes with the baby thoughts, I keep thinking what if I bring a kid in the world and I'm not successful enough to give them a better life...grrrr. Anyways...my goal today is living within the moment. I can think about the future but the minute I start to feel stressed I will work on snapping myself back. I think maybe I stress about the future so much because of my self-confidence. Deep down inside I could possibly be doubting myself. I wouldn't think that I do but maybe it's deeper than my own control and thoughts and I really fear it due to lack of confidence. Hopefully with me working on my confidence that'll fall into place. I wanna be confident in my natural state. Not just when my hair is done and I am dressed up. Or maybe I just never wanted anything more than

*to be successful....*deep breaths* "Change does not occur overnight."
When thoughts about quitting start to arise, me and my mind
have fights. I take control by reminding myself that quitting is no
option. It sounds good and may even sound better at the moment in
time, but it's no real option. Period.*

*P.S. I can support someone in my life who has recently stumbled,
by sharing my story, in hopes that it'll motivate them to get back
up..."*

Funny that you tell yourself change does not occur overnight,
but you will continue to work on this for years to come. We
spend so much time investing in the past and future that present
moments are often times hard to live within. Knowing that
change will not happen overnight will be something to really
learn, understand, and accept. It will take time no matter how
well you paint the picture of the outcome. Peace will come from
the ability to accept that everything will happen exactly how and
when it is supposed to, unless you get in the way. Find balance in
allowing things to be what they are, but still putting in enough
effort to fight for an outcome that is favored for you.

* * *

*05/18/2015: "It has been a few days since I last wrote. I have
been a tad bit busy. I saw my dad for the first time in 2 years. It
was wonderful. I enjoyed every bit of it. I cannot express how the
day in itself made me feel. I was so joyful, I spent time bonding
with my sisters and stepmom as we took a road trip and I learned
more about each of them than I have in 20 years. SO fun! Seeing
my dad was everything plus more. I cannot wait until he comes*

home. Like CANNOT wait. I wanted him to leave right there with us. It is so fortunate that me and my sisters have a dad like mine. I honestly feel as if I have the BEST dad ever. I love him. Other than that, seeing my family was great as usual. I love my family (in Chicago). No matter what the situation is, I always feel so good when I am around them. I realized this weekend that my happy place is with my family. I just love them so much, it's literally unconditional. So that is something I learned about myself, HOORAY! I have been consistently feeling good and I catch myself every time I'm leaning towards any negative emotion. I am nowhere near where I want to be but I definitely see progress within myself. I only want to think positive and I only want to be around positive things and people. I know that in the end it'll lead me to a happy life. So, I am going to continue on this journey, I know I can do it. One of my BIGGEST struggles right now is that when I am trying to think positive, I have a negative thought that just takes it overboard. Like it seems like the more positive I try to think, the more extreme the negative thought is. I HATE it. It literally drives me insane. I do not get why or how this "thought or voice" just thinks of the dumbest, meanest, things. It's thoughts that I wouldn't even think, thoughts that make me uncomfortable! Today was the first day I actually had to say out loud "shutup, I don't want to think like that. That's not me, its childish, etc." I hope that after writing this I see it less, normally when I write things it works out. I have been happy with Desmond. So happy that my baby fever is sneaking back on me. My dad approves of baby fever because he wants a "thing" to take care of lol. So I am not as scared and I don't really have any major stipulations on getting pregnant. Well

I just wanted to make note that I am happy and I hope to stay this way!!!"

* * *

05/29/2015: "My anxiety is raging through the roof right now. I have been doing so good in my relationship, so happy, so nice, so willing and it seems as if the universe is trying to tell me that he is not the one that is deserving of the woman that I am trying to become. For all the positiveness I give off, I swear he gives of 100 times more negative energy. I am so ready to call it quits with this man. We have been trying to get pregnant. All week, I have been stepping out of my comfort zone and allowing him to be a part of my happiness. & today, as it never fails, he pissed me off. I whole heartedly believe that he is not the one for me. I want him to be. He does make me happy and we do have great times together, but when he does something bad, it's like the absolute dumbest thing a person could do. It kills me. My heart aches like it did in 08-09. My feelings are so hurt because I wanna love him, I wanna be with him, and I want him to be the one. I enjoy our happy times. I wish things could be that all the time, but sheesh. I am officially losing hope in him being a part of my happiness. I see so much progression in myself, I see so many different things that I am just loving about myself. All for him to keep taking me back to a girl I no longer want to be. Disrespectful, angry, and crazy. The girl whose head spins and vomits out green throw up. I literally want nothing to do with her. To go so many days being so happy, it hurts me to be upset. This upset. I do not know what to do. But I will figure it out. Sooner than later."

He is not the problem. Your friends are not the problem. Nor are your family members the problem. The problem is you putting your happiness and sanity in the hands of others to handle when it belongs to you. Take the blame away from those around you and take accountability for your own happiness. The sooner you learn this, as with all advice given, the sooner you will achieve the goal that you are constantly chasing after. You are making this about him because you do not yet realize that you are the only person in control of your emotions. It is not fair to anyone you love to make them responsible for your emotions. Whatever situation led you to writing this entry is one that you cannot even almost remember. This is confirmation that it was not the situation and/or the person. Work on controlling and being responsible for your own emotions.

* * *

06/04/2015: *"My anxiety is at an all-time high. I wish it calms tf down lol. Well today's topic revolves around my relationships with people. I want to say that today is the last day I will let the actions of others affect me. The only thing is, I don't know if I will be able to hold my word to that. I will start off with friends. I hope to keep my circle small and to stop letting people who I know aren't the same as me, upset me. Tish made me very upset. I try and I try because I know at one point in time I could get with her, but as I am growing up and she is growing up, I really just do not like the person that she is panning out to be. It may be appealing to the eyes of others and I am not naming it wrong, but I just cannot. I would prefer to keep it at a distance with her and that's that. She has proven time and time again that she will never be who I wanted her to or who she once appeared to be. I am going to accept it and try to keep it moving. My mother. I don't even feel like writing about her because I have written the same things over for years. I appreciate the woman who she is attempting to become, but the real her always surfaces just in time to let me know what it is. I love her, but it's another relationship that I would prefer to keep at a distance. We just do not rock and I don't see it happening. We are two completely different people with too many of the same qualities if that makes any sense. I just wanna wash my hands with anyone who brings me ill feelings or negativity. I am making it a goal of mine to learn how to love at a distance. Well today I am taking another pregnancy test just to be 100% sure that I am not pregnant. I am praying it turns out negative and that I get the positive that I want in the next couple weeks to confirm that me and Desmond will be parents. I have never been this excited about a baby, since the fever swept over me last year. Welp, when I test I will be updating, so look out for good news!! I am still working on myself and I see progress every day. I feel like I hit a rough spot, almost forgetting the goal, but I quickly remembered what I set myself out to do last month. Still at it!!"*

* * *

06/12/2015: "I do not know what I feel tonight, but my mind is racing. My brother is in the ICU with pneumonia, I hate that I have to cut so many people off, my stretch marks are making me want to cry, I'm craving to see what my future will be, mad at myself for ever taking Desmond for granted, my mom will never admit in full truth to her wrongdoings, and I am just flat out annoyed. Tonight is definitely a rough one, but I do want to turn it around. I want to think happy thoughts and I want to feel happy. I hate these spells. I hope one day I can completely get over them. I just get completely sad about everything and want to hide in a closet. It's an unpleasant feeling. It truly is. Today Desmond said he notices a change in my attitude and I'm more pleasant to be around, that made me happy. I wonder where all this emotion stems from. Sometimes I don't get it. I love the fact that writing can help the feeling though. I always feel much better when I write. I think, and just think I am not for sure. I think that I'm not feeling happy with myself. Why? absolutely no clue. It's almost like I'm mad at myself, but I do not know why. It sounds crazy but when I deleted my Facebook I did not get this feeling. Maybe I got too deep into Facebook again? I don't know. I just want to figure it out. Welp, I am at work, so I know I won't have a break down, but I want sunshine. I did forget to remind myself that "I am having a good day."

Also the negative thoughts have come back, maybe that has something to do with me not mentally talking to myself as much as I was about a month ago. I have to get back to that because the negative thoughts drive me insane. I need them to stop, it is like having two minds. The sh*t is beyond annoying. Like I cannot put into words how annoying it is. I am just an emotional wreck tonight, grrr. I want to cuddle my boyfriend and fall asleep right now. That's all I want."

* * *

09/21/2015: "I have been putting off writing for weeks. It's like during the times where I know I NEED to write, I just cannot bring myself to do it. I don't know what it is. Maybe I'm afraid of being honest with myself? I guess I just really don't know. I should *give myself a 30 day trial. I feel better already and I haven't even wrote sh*t down. My 30 day challenge should be to write every day. Even if it is a sentence. Anyhow, my life, my life, my f*cking life. It's so dumb as of now. There are a lot of things I have to be thankful for, but there are a lot of things that I want to put in the toilet and flush. Let's start with my mom going to jail, the week my junior year in college starts. Leaving two little boys in my care. I am so fed up with her bullsh*t. So, I went and filed for guardianship in which I have court for next month. I am stuck in between not wanting to do it and just doing it. Like I have every reason to do it, but being the caring person I am, I keep worrying about her feelings and how it may make her feel. She is not the parent I want her to be for them. & while writing this I just thought about it, I need to do this. I keep doubting myself, and scaring myself into believing that I'm not fit for the job. BUT I am. I am fit for the job and I can do this. I can do this just as long as Desmond is by my side. I believe that he will stick through it and stay by my side, but of course my conscious is always preparing me for the worst. My mind is all over the place because I don't know what's gonna happen. My mind is trying to prepare me for all possibilities, but I hate it. I want to just live in the day, focus on the day, and let tomorrow worry about tomorrow. That is one of the biggest things I struggle with and I have to remember to make that my answer in my next interview when they ask, "What are 3 of your worst qualities?" I worry about the future too much. So hard to focus on the day at hand. I'm gonna test myself on that too. See if I can stop frying my brain with next year's problems.*

Now on to work. I like my job a lot. But I'm always wondering about other opportunities, other experiences, and more for myself. I think part of the problem ties back into me being so worried about the future. I wonder what can help me with that. To just stop. Think about today and live in today. My job is good for me right now. For a college student it's really good for me. I get annoyed with co-workers, my boss can be irra, and I could make more but I can also make it work. Those are all things that I'll probably deal with for the rest of my working days. I am always thinking about 5 months ahead of time and I think that is causing a lot of funk in my brain. I need to re-focus. A degree is the goal and work and money will come with that. Hopefully after my 30 day trial I can overcome this terrible trait that I carry. School is good, but with everything else it's been extremely hard to focus. This week is going a little better than previous and I am hoping that it only gets better with time. I have been having a hard time completing things on time and also just listening and learning. It's like I am in school, but I am not in school at the same time. I know I can get it together so there's another goal. I have to do well this semester. That's what I set out to do and I'm going to. In class I'm thinking of a hundred different things and that again ties into worrying about what'll happen next. Seems to be a trend here. So I know what the biggest goal is here. With school I just want to focus more than anything. I'm fighting a battle in my head though. That's a huge problem as well. Because I'll tell myself to stop thinking about things, but negativity is just screaming. How do you overcome that negative voice that is always louder than your true self? I try. I guess I can try a little harder, and seek a little outside help maybe? My negative voice makes me want to die. It's just always so loud and stern and consistent. I just want it to go away. Like my true self doesn't want you here, we don't believe the same things, and you're just *annoying. Like when I'm reading, when I'm sitting, or when I'm alone...That voice goes to f*cking town. I hate it. So much. When I say it makes me want to die? I mean that in the most literal way I can possibly mean it. I feel good. I feel better. Glad to get some of this stuff out, but it's not even half yet. To add on the thoughts, they're not only negative. Some of them are really sick. That makes me want to die more so than the negative ones. What I don't get is how I can have two completely different minds thinking completely different sh*t. It's so dumb. So I'm gonna take some measures to get rid of the dumb f*cking sick voice. I have been wondering what the f*ck I wanna do with my life, but that stops at that line. I already know the answer and I have stated it many times throughout this entry. FOCUS ON THE NOW. I don't wanna see, visualize, or know what I wanna do with my life. Right now I like criminal justice, and right now I'm gonna earn a criminal justice degree. I'm gonna continue to work at Hope and continue to care for my brothers. I'm gonna continue trying to be the best sister and girlfriend to my boys, and I'm gonna enjoy life when I can. I'm gonna relax and think about all the things I have to be grateful for. I'm gonna smoke and drink wine when I feel like being under the influence. I'm gonna pay my bills, save what I can, and be happy when I'm broke. I'm gonna cry when I feel sad and laugh when I'm happy. I'm gonna surround myself with genuine things and people and separate myself from anything less than. Without hard feelings, because I know everyone isn't built the same. I'm gonna be happy with what life gives me and make the most of the things that I CANNOT CHANGE. I am gonna continue to find myself and accept that at 20 I don't know who or what I wanna be. I'm gonna be 20 years old, even if life has dogged me into a 50 year* *old woman who has been through hell, its counterparts, and back. I'm gonna continue working on being a good person inside and out. I'm gonna get dressed when I feel like it and bum around when I feel like it, even if that's 6 days a week. I'm gonna workout when I have the time and energy & when I can't I'm not gonna dwell on it because it's not life or death. I'm gonna try to lead a healthy life, but when I wanna indulge in the fattest sh*t...that is what I am going to f*cking do. Because I am tired. I'm tired of this life that I am creating myself. & I say myself because I am letting life beat on and define me. When I wanna take the PTO that I'VE EARNED to lay in bed and watch TV, you guessed it. That's what I'm going to do. When I wanna skip class...I'ma get my a** up and go to class cause I NEED MY DEGREE! That is my goal and that's where my focus should lay. Hopefully letting my thoughts out help me. I genuinely want the help these days. Even if it's from myself. I have created a support system and wrote it out. For a visual. When you're going through hard times, you realize who's there for you, who's always been there, and who's always going to be there. I have to say I am not surprised at the outcome. I wanna be. BUT sadly, I am not. I like the system that I visually filled out for myself. I'm happy with those people and I want them to be lifetime. I hope the list doesn't change for the worst. I hope people stay in their places or move in positive directions. I don't want anyone to fall off. I mentioned a while ago that I would like to be 100% honest with myself. Something else to go with that, is that I have noticed that if I can't be completely honest with myself. I can't be completely honest with anyone. So I am still working on that. & accepting everything for what it truly is. That is a big one for me that I would like to see pan out."*

Chapter 5: Let's Heal; Present Day

05/03/2020: In the beginning you may or may not be able to understand what it is that life is walking you through. You may have many questions or you may just create a barrier so strong that it appears you "do not care" what is happening around you. Throughout time you have created this mindset that you are alone. You feel as if you are the only one going though whatever it is that you may be experiencing. Whatever it is that you are feeling, you should know that you are nowhere near alone. Regardless of your story looking different than the person next to you or a stranger, you are not alone. We are all subject to life and it's lessons, regardless of how harsh or soft they may appear to be. Above all, remember that these lessons will only be as hard as you allow them to be. The only thing that you should focus on throughout this journey of yours, is maintaining your strength. Strength to continue through what anyone else would find intimidating. Strength to support yourself in moments you feel that you have nobody. Strength to be different, to be there for others, and most importantly, strength to be there for yourself how you want someone else to. In addition to strength, keep allowing yourself to grow. You will outgrow so many things within your mindset alone. When things no longer feel fulfilling or right, follow that. Follow the uncomfortable feelings until you reach a point of complete bliss and peace.

It isn't coincidental that your last entry of these journals end with you attempting to accept all things for what they are. As I bring you this response, I find myself in a similar space. Not just trying to accept things for what they are, but also trying to master living in the present moment. This will become a strength throughout time, to be acknowledged as one of the most important, for controlling emotions and thought processes. Staying in the present moment may not be at the top of 'things to learn' for you, but the sooner the better. When you understand that everything is happening exactly how and when it is supposed to, your healing process will become even easier. It will hurt as long as you are living in the past and future.

Despite how they were delivered to you, all of these were lessons of yours to learn. This story has been developing for over a decade and lessons will continue to repeat themselves until learned. While most of these things were accompanied by pain, the most important factor is that you understand that you were chosen. Being able to understand and accept this will come with the space you will eventually find yourself in life. Understand that every moment is the right time for you to continue growth, the right time for you to acknowledge and accept the past, the right time for you to let go of what the future may hold, the right time for you to be there for yourself, and the right time for you to beat anything that may have felt like a defeat in the past. We all embody the trait to live and enjoy what life brings to us in every moment. Being chosen means not only living and enjoying, but also learning and hurting throughout some of those moments.

Healing is and will continue to be a long term process. Let go of the false notion that at the point of acknowledgment, that is the same point of being completely healed. Trying to make sense of what life is trying to teach you, will be confusing at times. You will be led to believe that the healing process should be done when you realize what it is that you are going through. It will take so much more. More time, experience, and learning before a healed space is reached. Allow these situations to be what they are in the moment and seek ways to move beyond them after they have passed. Disfunction and lack of comfortability happens at the point that you fight or go against where life is naturally guiding you. Some of the lessons will be harder than others, some will hurt more, and some will not make as much sense. Look beyond what you see and accept them all. Let go of the idea that you have or will figure it all out as this story is not yet complete...

About The Author

Author Imani Watson was born in Chicago, IL and raised in Kalamazoo, MI. She began writing at 14 years old and continues to journal and blog today. Imani holds a Bachelor's Degree from Grand Valley State University and a Master's Degree from Clark Atlanta University. She is also the founder of 501(c)(3) Nonprofit Mommy's Break Inc.

Connect with Imani at https://imaniwatson.com/

CPSIA information can be obtained
at www.ICGtesting.com
Printed in the USA
JSHW021145211220
10439JS00004B/15

9 781735 954806